I0330906

C-611 CAREER EXAMINATION SERIES

This is your
PASSBOOK *for...*

Principal Clerk

Test Preparation Study Guide
Questions & Answers

NLC®

NATIONAL LEARNING CORPORATION®

National Learning Corporation

212 Michael Drive, Syosset, NY 11791
(516) 921-8888 • www.passbooks.com
E-mail: info@passbooks.com

PUBLISHED IN THE UNITED STATES OF AMERICA

PASSBOOK® SERIES

THE *PASSBOOK® SERIES* has been created to prepare applicants and candidates for the ultimate academic battlefield – the examination room.

At some time in our lives, each and every one of us may be required to take an examination – for validation, matriculation, admission, qualification, registration, certification, or licensure.

Based on the assumption that every applicant or candidate has met the basic formal educational standards, has taken the required number of courses, and read the necessary texts, the *PASSBOOK® SERIES* furnishes the one special preparation which may assure passing with confidence, instead of failing with insecurity. Examination questions – together with answers – are furnished as the basic vehicle for study so that the mysteries of the examination and its compounding difficulties may be eliminated or diminished by a sure method.

This book is meant to help you pass your examination provided that you qualify and are serious in your objective.

The entire field is reviewed through the huge store of content information which is succinctly presented through a provocative and challenging approach – the question-and-answer method.

A climate of success is established by furnishing the correct answers at the end of each test.

You soon learn to recognize types of questions, forms of questions, and patterns of questioning. You may even begin to anticipate expected outcomes.

You perceive that many questions are repeated or adapted so that you can gain acute insights, which may enable you to score many sure points.

You learn how to confront new questions, or types of questions, and to attack them confidently and work out the correct answers.

You note objectives and emphases, and recognize pitfalls and dangers, so that you may make positive educational adjustments.

Moreover, you are kept fully informed in relation to new concepts, methods, practices, and directions in the field.

You discover that you are actually taking the examination all the time: you are preparing for the examination by "taking" an examination, not by reading extraneous and/or supererogatory textbooks.

In short, this PASSBOOK®, used directedly, should be an important factor in helping you to pass your test.

PRINCIPAL CLERK

DUTIES

The employee in this class performs highly difficult and responsible clerical functions of a varied nature and/or supervises a unit of employees performing specialized clerical duties. Supervision may be exercised over subordinate supervisory and clerical employees engaged in maintaining a large number of clerical records requiring complex procedures. Employees are held responsible for the proper performance of the assigned supervisory or technical activities of their unit and they make independent work decisions based on experience and knowledge of departmental operations. Difficult technical policy and procedural questions are referred to a supervisor for decision. Work is reviewed through conferences, audits and observations of administrative supervisors. Performs related work as required.

SCOPE OF THE EXAMINATION

The written test will cover knowledge, skills, and/or abilities in such areas as:

1. Understanding and interpreting written material;
2. Supervision;
3. English usage, sentence structure, grammar, spelling, and punctuation;
4. Basic computer usage;
5. Interpreting data in record keeping; and
6. Clerical operations.

HOW TO TAKE A TEST

I. YOU MUST PASS AN EXAMINATION

A. WHAT EVERY CANDIDATE SHOULD KNOW

Examination applicants often ask us for help in preparing for the written test. What can I study in advance? What kinds of questions will be asked? How will the test be given? How will the papers be graded?

As an applicant for a civil service examination, you may be wondering about some of these things. Our purpose here is to suggest effective methods of advance study and to describe civil service examinations.

Your chances for success on this examination can be increased if you know how to prepare. Those "pre-examination jitters" can be reduced if you know what to expect. You can even experience an adventure in good citizenship if you know why civil service exams are given.

B. WHY ARE CIVIL SERVICE EXAMINATIONS GIVEN?

Civil service examinations are important to you in two ways. As a citizen, you want public jobs filled by employees who know how to do their work. As a job seeker, you want a fair chance to compete for that job on an equal footing with other candidates. The best-known means of accomplishing this two-fold goal is the competitive examination.

Exams are widely publicized throughout the nation. They may be administered for jobs in federal, state, city, municipal, town or village governments or agencies.

Any citizen may apply, with some limitations, such as the age or residence of applicants. Your experience and education may be reviewed to see whether you meet the requirements for the particular examination. When these requirements exist, they are reasonable and applied consistently to all applicants. Thus, a competitive examination may cause you some uneasiness now, but it is your privilege and safeguard.

C. HOW ARE CIVIL SERVICE EXAMS DEVELOPED?

Examinations are carefully written by trained technicians who are specialists in the field known as "psychological measurement," in consultation with recognized authorities in the field of work that the test will cover. These experts recommend the subject matter areas or skills to be tested; only those knowledges or skills important to your success on the job are included. The most reliable books and source materials available are used as references. Together, the experts and technicians judge the difficulty level of the questions.

Test technicians know how to phrase questions so that the problem is clearly stated. Their ethics do not permit "trick" or "catch" questions. Questions may have been tried out on sample groups, or subjected to statistical analysis, to determine their usefulness.

Written tests are often used in combination with performance tests, ratings of training and experience, and oral interviews. All of these measures combine to form the best-known means of finding the right person for the right job.

II. HOW TO PASS THE WRITTEN TEST

A. NATURE OF THE EXAMINATION

To prepare intelligently for civil service examinations, you should know how they differ from school examinations you have taken. In school you were assigned certain definite pages to read or subjects to cover. The examination questions were quite detailed and usually emphasized memory. Civil service exams, on the other hand, try to discover your present ability to perform the duties of a position, plus your potentiality to learn these duties. In other words, a civil service exam attempts to predict how successful you will be. Questions cover such a broad area that they cannot be as minute and detailed as school exam questions.

In the public service similar kinds of work, or positions, are grouped together in one "class." This process is known as *position-classification.* All the positions in a class are paid according to the salary range for that class. One class title covers all of these positions, and they are all tested by the same examination.

B. FOUR BASIC STEPS

1) Study the announcement

How, then, can you know what subjects to study? Our best answer is: "Learn as much as possible about the class of positions for which you've applied." The exam will test the knowledge, skills and abilities needed to do the work.

Your most valuable source of information about the position you want is the official exam announcement. This announcement lists the training and experience qualifications. Check these standards and apply only if you come reasonably close to meeting them.

The brief description of the position in the examination announcement offers some clues to the subjects which will be tested. Think about the job itself. Review the duties in your mind. Can you perform them, or are there some in which you are rusty? Fill in the blank spots in your preparation.

Many jurisdictions preview the written test in the exam announcement by including a section called "Knowledge and Abilities Required," "Scope of the Examination," or some similar heading. Here you will find out specifically what fields will be tested.

2) Review your own background

Once you learn in general what the position is all about, and what you need to know to do the work, ask yourself which subjects you already know fairly well and which need improvement. You may wonder whether to concentrate on improving your strong areas or on building some background in your fields of weakness. When the announcement has specified "some knowledge" or "considerable knowledge," or has used adjectives like "beginning principles of..." or "advanced ... methods," you can get a clue as to the number and difficulty of questions to be asked in any given field. More questions, and hence broader coverage, would be included for those subjects which are more important in the work. Now weigh your strengths and weaknesses against the job requirements and prepare accordingly.

3) Determine the level of the position

Another way to tell how intensively you should prepare is to understand the level of the job for which you are applying. Is it the entering level? In other words, is this the position in which beginners in a field of work are hired? Or is it an intermediate or advanced level? Sometimes this is indicated by such words as "Junior" or "Senior" in the class title. Other jurisdictions use Roman numerals to designate the level – Clerk I, Clerk II, for example. The word "Supervisor" sometimes appears in the title. If the level is not indicated by the title, check the description of duties. Will you be working under very close supervision, or will you have responsibility for independent decisions in this work?

4) Choose appropriate study materials

Now that you know the subjects to be examined and the relative amount of each subject to be covered, you can choose suitable study materials. For beginning level jobs, or even advanced ones, if you have a pronounced weakness in some aspect of your training, read a modern, standard textbook in that field. Be sure it is up to date and has general coverage. Such books are normally available at your library, and the librarian will be glad to help you locate one. For entry-level positions, questions of appropriate difficulty are chosen – neither highly advanced questions, nor those too simple. Such questions require careful thought but not advanced training.

If the position for which you are applying is technical or advanced, you will read more advanced, specialized material. If you are already familiar with the basic principles of your field, elementary textbooks would waste your time. Concentrate on advanced textbooks and technical periodicals. Think through the concepts and review difficult problems in your field.

These are all general sources. You can get more ideas on your own initiative, following these leads. For example, training manuals and publications of the government agency which employs workers in your field can be useful, particularly for technical and professional positions. A letter or visit to the government department involved may result in more specific study suggestions, and certainly will provide you with a more definite idea of the exact nature of the position you are seeking.

III. KINDS OF TESTS

Tests are used for purposes other than measuring knowledge and ability to perform specified duties. For some positions, it is equally important to test ability to make adjustments to new situations or to profit from training. In others, basic mental abilities not dependent on information are essential. Questions which test these things may not appear as pertinent to the duties of the position as those which test for knowledge and information. Yet they are often highly important parts of a fair examination. For very general questions, it is almost impossible to help you direct your study efforts. What we can do is to point out some of the more common of these general abilities needed in public service positions and describe some typical questions.

1) General information

Broad, general information has been found useful for predicting job success in some kinds of work. This is tested in a variety of ways, from vocabulary lists to questions about current events. Basic background in some field of work, such as sociology or economics, may be sampled in a group of questions. Often these are principles which have become familiar to most persons through exposure rather than through formal training. It is difficult to advise you how to study for these questions; being alert to the world around you is our best suggestion.

2) Verbal ability

An example of an ability needed in many positions is verbal or language ability. Verbal ability is, in brief, the ability to use and understand words. Vocabulary and grammar tests are typical measures of this ability. Reading comprehension or paragraph interpretation questions are common in many kinds of civil service tests. You are given a paragraph of written material and asked to find its central meaning.

3) Numerical ability

Number skills can be tested by the familiar arithmetic problem, by checking paired lists of numbers to see which are alike and which are different, or by interpreting charts and graphs. In the latter test, a graph may be printed in the test booklet which you are asked to use as the basis for answering questions.

4) Observation

A popular test for law-enforcement positions is the observation test. A picture is shown to you for several minutes, then taken away. Questions about the picture test your ability to observe both details and larger elements.

5) Following directions

In many positions in the public service, the employee must be able to carry out written instructions dependably and accurately. You may be given a chart with several columns, each column listing a variety of information. The questions require you to carry out directions involving the information given in the chart.

6) Skills and aptitudes

Performance tests effectively measure some manual skills and aptitudes. When the skill is one in which you are trained, such as typing or shorthand, you can practice. These tests are often very much like those given in business school or high school courses. For many of the other skills and aptitudes, however, no short-time preparation can be made. Skills and abilities natural to you or that you have developed throughout your lifetime are being tested.

Many of the general questions just described provide all the data needed to answer the questions and ask you to use your reasoning ability to find the answers. Your best preparation for these tests, as well as for tests of facts and ideas, is to be at your physical and mental best. You, no doubt, have your own methods of getting into an exam-taking mood and keeping "in shape." The next section lists some ideas on this subject.

IV. KINDS OF QUESTIONS

Only rarely is the "essay" question, which you answer in narrative form, used in civil service tests. Civil service tests are usually of the short-answer type. Full instructions for answering these questions will be given to you at the examination. But in case this is your first experience with short-answer questions and separate answer sheets, here is what you need to know:

1) Multiple-choice Questions

Most popular of the short-answer questions is the "multiple choice" or "best answer" question. It can be used, for example, to test for factual knowledge, ability to solve problems or judgment in meeting situations found at work.

A multiple-choice question is normally one of three types—

- It can begin with an incomplete statement followed by several possible endings. You are to find the one ending which *best* completes the statement, although some of the others may not be entirely wrong.
- It can also be a complete statement in the form of a question which is answered by choosing one of the statements listed.

- It can be in the form of a problem – again you select the best answer.

Here is an example of a multiple-choice question with a discussion which should give you some clues as to the method for choosing the right answer:

When an employee has a complaint about his assignment, the action which will *best* help him overcome his difficulty is to
A. discuss his difficulty with his coworkers
B. take the problem to the head of the organization
C. take the problem to the person who gave him the assignment
D. say nothing to anyone about his complaint

In answering this question, you should study each of the choices to find which is best. Consider choice "A" – Certainly an employee may discuss his complaint with fellow employees, but no change or improvement can result, and the complaint remains unresolved. Choice "B" is a poor choice since the head of the organization probably does not know what assignment you have been given, and taking your problem to him is known as "going over the head" of the supervisor. The supervisor, or person who made the assignment, is the person who can clarify it or correct any injustice. Choice "C" is, therefore, correct. To say nothing, as in choice "D," is unwise. Supervisors have and interest in knowing the problems employees are facing, and the employee is seeking a solution to his problem.

2) True/False Questions

The "true/false" or "right/wrong" form of question is sometimes used. Here a complete statement is given. Your job is to decide whether the statement is right or wrong.

SAMPLE: A roaming cell-phone call to a nearby city costs less than a non-roaming call to a distant city.

This statement is wrong, or false, since roaming calls are more expensive.

This is not a complete list of all possible question forms, although most of the others are variations of these common types. You will always get complete directions for answering questions. Be sure you understand *how* to mark your answers – ask questions until you do.

V. RECORDING YOUR ANSWERS

Computer terminals are used more and more today for many different kinds of exams.

For an examination with very few applicants, you may be told to record your answers in the test booklet itself. Separate answer sheets are much more common. If this separate answer sheet is to be scored by machine – and this is often the case – it is highly important that you mark your answers correctly in order to get credit.

An electronic scoring machine is often used in civil service offices because of the speed with which papers can be scored. Machine-scored answer sheets must be marked with a pencil, which will be given to you. This pencil has a high graphite content which responds to the electronic scoring machine. As a matter of fact, stray dots may register as answers, so do not let your pencil rest on the answer sheet while you are pondering the correct answer. Also, if your pencil lead breaks or is otherwise defective, ask for another.

Since the answer sheet will be dropped in a slot in the scoring machine, be careful not to bend the corners or get the paper crumpled.

The answer sheet normally has five vertical columns of numbers, with 30 numbers to a column. These numbers correspond to the question numbers in your test booklet. After each number, going across the page are four or five pairs of dotted lines. These short dotted lines have small letters or numbers above them. The first two pairs may also have a "T" or "F" above the letters. This indicates that the first two pairs only are to be used if the questions are of the true-false type. If the questions are multiple choice, disregard the "T" and "F" and pay attention only to the small letters or numbers.

Answer your questions in the manner of the sample that follows:

32. The largest city in the United States is
    A. Washington, D.C.
    B. New York City
    C. Chicago
    D. Detroit
    E. San Francisco

1) Choose the answer you think is best. (New York City is the largest, so "B" is correct.)
2) Find the row of dotted lines numbered the same as the question you are answering. (Find row number 32)
3) Find the pair of dotted lines corresponding to the answer. (Find the pair of lines under the mark "B.")
4) Make a solid black mark between the dotted lines.

VI. BEFORE THE TEST

Common sense will help you find procedures to follow to get ready for an examination. Too many of us, however, overlook these sensible measures. Indeed, nervousness and fatigue have been found to be the most serious reasons why applicants fail to do their best on civil service tests. Here is a list of reminders:

- Begin your preparation early – Don't wait until the last minute to go scurrying around for books and materials or to find out what the position is all about.
- Prepare continuously – An hour a night for a week is better than an all-night cram session. This has been definitely established. What is more, a night a week for a month will return better dividends than crowding your study into a shorter period of time.
- Locate the place of the exam – You have been sent a notice telling you when and where to report for the examination. If the location is in a different town or otherwise unfamiliar to you, it would be well to inquire the best route and learn something about the building.
- Relax the night before the test – Allow your mind to rest. Do not study at all that night. Plan some mild recreation or diversion; then go to bed early and get a good night's sleep.
- Get up early enough to make a leisurely trip to the place for the test – This way unforeseen events, traffic snarls, unfamiliar buildings, etc. will not upset you.
- Dress comfortably – A written test is not a fashion show. You will be known by number and not by name, so wear something comfortable.

- Leave excess paraphernalia at home – Shopping bags and odd bundles will get in your way. You need bring only the items mentioned in the official notice you received; usually everything you need is provided. Do not bring reference books to the exam. They will only confuse those last minutes and be taken away from you when in the test room.
- Arrive somewhat ahead of time – If because of transportation schedules you must get there very early, bring a newspaper or magazine to take your mind off yourself while waiting.
- Locate the examination room – When you have found the proper room, you will be directed to the seat or part of the room where you will sit. Sometimes you are given a sheet of instructions to read while you are waiting. Do not fill out any forms until you are told to do so; just read them and be prepared.
- Relax and prepare to listen to the instructions
- If you have any physical problem that may keep you from doing your best, be sure to tell the test administrator. If you are sick or in poor health, you really cannot do your best on the exam. You can come back and take the test some other time.

VII. AT THE TEST

The day of the test is here and you have the test booklet in your hand. The temptation to get going is very strong. Caution! There is more to success than knowing the right answers. You must know how to identify your papers and understand variations in the type of short-answer question used in this particular examination. Follow these suggestions for maximum results from your efforts:

1) Cooperate with the monitor

The test administrator has a duty to create a situation in which you can be as much at ease as possible. He will give instructions, tell you when to begin, check to see that you are marking your answer sheet correctly, and so on. He is not there to guard you, although he will see that your competitors do not take unfair advantage. He wants to help you do your best.

2) Listen to all instructions

Don't jump the gun! Wait until you understand all directions. In most civil service tests you get more time than you need to answer the questions. So don't be in a hurry. Read each word of instructions until you clearly understand the meaning. Study the examples, listen to all announcements and follow directions. Ask questions if you do not understand what to do.

3) Identify your papers

Civil service exams are usually identified by number only. You will be assigned a number; you must not put your name on your test papers. Be sure to copy your number correctly. Since more than one exam may be given, copy your exact examination title.

4) Plan your time

Unless you are told that a test is a "speed" or "rate of work" test, speed itself is usually not important. Time enough to answer all the questions will be provided, but this does not mean that you have all day. An overall time limit has been set. Divide the total time (in minutes) by the number of questions to determine the approximate time you have for each question.

5) Do not linger over difficult questions

If you come across a difficult question, mark it with a paper clip (useful to have along) and come back to it when you have been through the booklet. One caution if you do this – be sure to skip a number on your answer sheet as well. Check often to be sure that you have not lost your place and that you are marking in the row numbered the same as the question you are answering.

6) Read the questions

Be sure you know what the question asks! Many capable people are unsuccessful because they failed to *read* the questions correctly.

7) Answer all questions

Unless you have been instructed that a penalty will be deducted for incorrect answers, it is better to guess than to omit a question.

8) Speed tests

It is often better NOT to guess on speed tests. It has been found that on timed tests people are tempted to spend the last few seconds before time is called in marking answers at random – without even reading them – in the hope of picking up a few extra points. To discourage this practice, the instructions may warn you that your score will be "corrected" for guessing. That is, a penalty will be applied. The incorrect answers will be deducted from the correct ones, or some other penalty formula will be used.

9) Review your answers

If you finish before time is called, go back to the questions you guessed or omitted to give them further thought. Review other answers if you have time.

10) Return your test materials

If you are ready to leave before others have finished or time is called, take ALL your materials to the monitor and leave quietly. Never take any test material with you. The monitor can discover whose papers are not complete, and taking a test booklet may be grounds for disqualification.

VIII. EXAMINATION TECHNIQUES

1) Read the general instructions carefully. These are usually printed on the first page of the exam booklet. As a rule, these instructions refer to the timing of the examination; the fact that you should not start work until the signal and must stop work at a signal, etc. If there are any *special* instructions, such as a choice of questions to be answered, make sure that you note this instruction carefully.

2) When you are ready to start work on the examination, that is as soon as the signal has been given, read the instructions to each question booklet, underline any key words or phrases, such as *least, best, outline, describe* and the like. In this way you will tend to answer as requested rather than discover on reviewing your paper that you *listed without describing*, that you selected the *worst* choice rather than the *best* choice, etc.

3) If the examination is of the objective or multiple-choice type – that is, each question will also give a series of possible answers: A, B, C or D, and you are called upon to select the best answer and write the letter next to that answer on your answer paper – it is advisable to start answering each question in turn. There may be anywhere from 50 to 100 such questions in the three or four hours allotted and you can see how much time would be taken if you read through all the questions before beginning to answer any. Furthermore, if you come across a question or group of questions which you know would be difficult to answer, it would undoubtedly affect your handling of all the other questions.

4) If the examination is of the essay type and contains but a few questions, it is a moot point as to whether you should read all the questions before starting to answer any one. Of course, if you are given a choice – say five out of seven and the like – then it is essential to read all the questions so you can eliminate the two that are most difficult. If, however, you are asked to answer all the questions, there may be danger in trying to answer the easiest one first because you may find that you will spend too much time on it. The best technique is to answer the first question, then proceed to the second, etc.

5) Time your answers. Before the exam begins, write down the time it started, then add the time allowed for the examination and write down the time it must be completed, then divide the time available somewhat as follows:
   - If 3-1/2 hours are allowed, that would be 210 minutes. If you have 80 objective-type questions, that would be an average of 2-1/2 minutes per question. Allow yourself no more than 2 minutes per question, or a total of 160 minutes, which will permit about 50 minutes to review.
   - If for the time allotment of 210 minutes there are 7 essay questions to answer, that would average about 30 minutes a question. Give yourself only 25 minutes per question so that you have about 35 minutes to review.

6) The most important instruction is to *read each question* and make sure you know what is wanted. The second most important instruction is to *time yourself properly* so that you answer every question. The third most important instruction is to *answer every question*. Guess if you have to but include something for each question. Remember that you will receive no credit for a blank and will probably receive some credit if you write something in answer to an essay question. If you guess a letter – say "B" for a multiple-choice question – you may have guessed right. If you leave a blank as an answer to a multiple-choice question, the examiners may respect your feelings but it will not add a point to your score. Some exams may penalize you for wrong answers, so in such cases *only*, you may not want to guess unless you have some basis for your answer.

7) Suggestions
   a. Objective-type questions
      1. Examine the question booklet for proper sequence of pages and questions
      2. Read all instructions carefully
      3. Skip any question which seems too difficult; return to it after all other questions have been answered
      4. Apportion your time properly; do not spend too much time on any single question or group of questions

5. Note and underline key words – *all, most, fewest, least, best, worst, same, opposite,* etc.
6. Pay particular attention to negatives
7. Note unusual option, e.g., unduly long, short, complex, different or similar in content to the body of the question
8. Observe the use of "hedging" words – *probably, may, most likely,* etc.
9. Make sure that your answer is put next to the same number as the question
10. Do not second-guess unless you have good reason to believe the second answer is definitely more correct
11. Cross out original answer if you decide another answer is more accurate; do not erase until you are ready to hand your paper in
12. Answer all questions; guess unless instructed otherwise
13. Leave time for review

b. Essay questions
1. Read each question carefully
2. Determine exactly what is wanted. Underline key words or phrases.
3. Decide on outline or paragraph answer
4. Include many different points and elements unless asked to develop any one or two points or elements
5. Show impartiality by giving pros and cons unless directed to select one side only
6. Make and write down any assumptions you find necessary to answer the questions
7. Watch your English, grammar, punctuation and choice of words
8. Time your answers; don't crowd material

8) Answering the essay question

Most essay questions can be answered by framing the specific response around several key words or ideas. Here are a few such key words or ideas:

M's: manpower, materials, methods, money, management
P's: purpose, program, policy, plan, procedure, practice, problems, pitfalls, personnel, public relations

a. Six basic steps in handling problems:
1. Preliminary plan and background development
2. Collect information, data and facts
3. Analyze and interpret information, data and facts
4. Analyze and develop solutions as well as make recommendations
5. Prepare report and sell recommendations
6. Install recommendations and follow up effectiveness

b. Pitfalls to avoid
1. *Taking things for granted* – A statement of the situation does not necessarily imply that each of the elements is necessarily true; for example, a complaint may be invalid and biased so that all that can be taken for granted is that a complaint has been registered

2. *Considering only one side of a situation* – Wherever possible, indicate several alternatives and then point out the reasons you selected the best one
3. *Failing to indicate follow up* – Whenever your answer indicates action on your part, make certain that you will take proper follow-up action to see how successful your recommendations, procedures or actions turn out to be
4. *Taking too long in answering any single question* – Remember to time your answers properly

IX. AFTER THE TEST

Scoring procedures differ in detail among civil service jurisdictions although the general principles are the same. Whether the papers are hand-scored or graded by machine we have described, they are nearly always graded by number. That is, the person who marks the paper knows only the number – never the name – of the applicant. Not until all the papers have been graded will they be matched with names. If other tests, such as training and experience or oral interview ratings have been given, scores will be combined. Different parts of the examination usually have different weights. For example, the written test might count 60 percent of the final grade, and a rating of training and experience 40 percent. In many jurisdictions, veterans will have a certain number of points added to their grades.

After the final grade has been determined, the names are placed in grade order and an eligible list is established. There are various methods for resolving ties between those who get the same final grade – probably the most common is to place first the name of the person whose application was received first. Job offers are made from the eligible list in the order the names appear on it. You will be notified of your grade and your rank as soon as all these computations have been made. This will be done as rapidly as possible.

People who are found to meet the requirements in the announcement are called "eligibles." Their names are put on a list of eligible candidates. An eligible's chances of getting a job depend on how high he stands on this list and how fast agencies are filling jobs from the list.

When a job is to be filled from a list of eligibles, the agency asks for the names of people on the list of eligibles for that job. When the civil service commission receives this request, it sends to the agency the names of the three people highest on this list. Or, if the job to be filled has specialized requirements, the office sends the agency the names of the top three persons who meet these requirements from the general list.

The appointing officer makes a choice from among the three people whose names were sent to him. If the selected person accepts the appointment, the names of the others are put back on the list to be considered for future openings.

That is the rule in hiring from all kinds of eligible lists, whether they are for typist, carpenter, chemist, or something else. For every vacancy, the appointing officer has his choice of any one of the top three eligibles on the list. This explains why the person whose name is on top of the list sometimes does not get an appointment when some of the persons lower on the list do. If the appointing officer chooses the second or third eligible, the No. 1 eligible does not get a job at once, but stays on the list until he is appointed or the list is terminated.

X. HOW TO PASS THE INTERVIEW TEST

The examination for which you applied requires an oral interview test. You have already taken the written test and you are now being called for the interview test – the final part of the formal examination.

You may think that it is not possible to prepare for an interview test and that there are no procedures to follow during an interview. Our purpose is to point out some things you can do in advance that will help you and some good rules to follow and pitfalls to avoid while you are being interviewed.

What is an interview supposed to test?

The written examination is designed to test the technical knowledge and competence of the candidate; the oral is designed to evaluate intangible qualities, not readily measured otherwise, and to establish a list showing the relative fitness of each candidate – as measured against his competitors – for the position sought. Scoring is not on the basis of "right" and "wrong," but on a sliding scale of values ranging from "not passable" to "outstanding." As a matter of fact, it is possible to achieve a relatively low score without a single "incorrect" answer because of evident weakness in the qualities being measured.

Occasionally, an examination may consist entirely of an oral test – either an individual or a group oral. In such cases, information is sought concerning the technical knowledges and abilities of the candidate, since there has been no written examination for this purpose. More commonly, however, an oral test is used to supplement a written examination.

Who conducts interviews?

The composition of oral boards varies among different jurisdictions. In nearly all, a representative of the personnel department serves as chairman. One of the members of the board may be a representative of the department in which the candidate would work. In some cases, "outside experts" are used, and, frequently, a businessman or some other representative of the general public is asked to serve. Labor and management or other special groups may be represented. The aim is to secure the services of experts in the appropriate field.

However the board is composed, it is a good idea (and not at all improper or unethical) to ascertain in advance of the interview who the members are and what groups they represent. When you are introduced to them, you will have some idea of their backgrounds and interests, and at least you will not stutter and stammer over their names.

What should be done before the interview?

While knowledge about the board members is useful and takes some of the surprise element out of the interview, there is other preparation which is more substantive. It *is* possible to prepare for an oral interview – in several ways:

1) Keep a copy of your application and review it carefully before the interview

This may be the only document before the oral board, and the starting point of the interview. Know what education and experience you have listed there, and the sequence and dates of all of it. Sometimes the board will ask you to review the highlights of your experience for them; you should not have to hem and haw doing it.

2) Study the class specification and the examination announcement

Usually, the oral board has one or both of these to guide them. The qualities, characteristics or knowledges required by the position sought are stated in these documents. They offer valuable clues as to the nature of the oral interview. For example, if the job involves supervisory responsibilities, the announcement will usually indicate that knowledge of modern supervisory methods and the qualifications of the candidate as a supervisor will be tested. If so, you can expect such questions, frequently in the form of a hypothetical situation which you are expected to solve. NEVER go into an oral without knowledge of the duties and responsibilities of the job you seek.

3) Think through each qualification required

Try to visualize the kind of questions you would ask if you were a board member. How well could you answer them? Try especially to appraise your own knowledge and background in each area, *measured against the job sought*, and identify any areas in which you are weak. Be critical and realistic – do not flatter yourself.

4) Do some general reading in areas in which you feel you may be weak

For example, if the job involves supervision and your past experience has NOT, some general reading in supervisory methods and practices, particularly in the field of human relations, might be useful. Do NOT study agency procedures or detailed manuals. The oral board will be testing your understanding and capacity, not your memory.

5) Get a good night's sleep and watch your general health and mental attitude

You will want a clear head at the interview. Take care of a cold or any other minor ailment, and of course, no hangovers.

What should be done on the day of the interview?

Now comes the day of the interview itself. Give yourself plenty of time to get there. Plan to arrive somewhat ahead of the scheduled time, particularly if your appointment is in the fore part of the day. If a previous candidate fails to appear, the board might be ready for you a bit early. By early afternoon an oral board is almost invariably behind schedule if there are many candidates, and you may have to wait. Take along a book or magazine to read, or your application to review, but leave any extraneous material in the waiting room when you go in for your interview. In any event, relax and compose yourself.

The matter of dress is important. The board is forming impressions about you – from your experience, your manners, your attitude, and your appearance. Give your personal appearance careful attention. Dress your best, but not your flashiest. Choose conservative, appropriate clothing, and be sure it is immaculate. This is a business interview, and your appearance should indicate that you regard it as such. Besides, being well groomed and properly dressed will help boost your confidence.

Sooner or later, someone will call your name and escort you into the interview room. *This is it.* From here on you are on your own. It is too late for any more preparation. But remember, you asked for this opportunity to prove your fitness, and you are here because your request was granted.

What happens when you go in?

The usual sequence of events will be as follows: The clerk (who is often the board stenographer) will introduce you to the chairman of the oral board, who will introduce you to the other members of the board. Acknowledge the introductions before you sit down. Do not be surprised if you find a microphone facing you or a stenotypist sitting by. Oral interviews are usually recorded in the event of an appeal or other review.

Usually the chairman of the board will open the interview by reviewing the highlights of your education and work experience from your application – primarily for the benefit of the other members of the board, as well as to get the material into the record. Do not interrupt or comment unless there is an error or significant misinterpretation; if that is the case, do not hesitate. But do not quibble about insignificant matters. Also, he will usually ask you some question about your education, experience or your present job – partly to get you to start talking and to establish the interviewing "rapport." He may start the actual questioning, or turn it over to one of the other members. Frequently, each member undertakes the questioning on a particular area, one in which he is perhaps most competent, so you can expect each member to participate in the examination. Because time is limited, you may also expect some rather abrupt switches in the direction the questioning takes, so do not be upset by it. Normally, a board member will not pursue a single line of questioning unless he discovers a particular strength or weakness.

After each member has participated, the chairman will usually ask whether any member has any further questions, then will ask you if you have anything you wish to add. Unless you are expecting this question, it may floor you. Worse, it may start you off on an extended, extemporaneous speech. The board is not usually seeking more information. The question is principally to offer you a last opportunity to present further qualifications or to indicate that you have nothing to add. So, if you feel that a significant qualification or characteristic has been overlooked, it is proper to point it out in a sentence or so. Do not compliment the board on the thoroughness of their examination – they have been sketchy, and you know it. If you wish, merely say, "No thank you, I have nothing further to add." This is a point where you can "talk yourself out" of a good impression or fail to present an important bit of information. Remember, *you close the interview yourself.*

The chairman will then say, "That is all, Mr. ______, thank you." Do not be startled; the interview is over, and quicker than you think. Thank him, gather your belongings and take your leave. Save your sigh of relief for the other side of the door.

How to put your best foot forward

Throughout this entire process, you may feel that the board individually and collectively is trying to pierce your defenses, seek out your hidden weaknesses and embarrass and confuse you. Actually, this is not true. They are obliged to make an appraisal of your qualifications for the job you are seeking, and they want to see you in your best light. Remember, they must interview all candidates and a non-cooperative candidate may become a failure in spite of their best efforts to bring out his qualifications. Here are 15 suggestions that will help you:

1) Be natural – Keep your attitude confident, not cocky

If you are not confident that you can do the job, do not expect the board to be. Do not apologize for your weaknesses, try to bring out your strong points. The board is interested in a positive, not negative, presentation. Cockiness will antagonize any board member and make him wonder if you are covering up a weakness by a false show of strength.

2) Get comfortable, but don't lounge or sprawl

Sit erectly but not stiffly. A careless posture may lead the board to conclude that you are careless in other things, or at least that you are not impressed by the importance of the occasion. Either conclusion is natural, even if incorrect. Do not fuss with your clothing, a pencil or an ashtray. Your hands may occasionally be useful to emphasize a point; do not let them become a point of distraction.

3) Do not wisecrack or make small talk

This is a serious situation, and your attitude should show that you consider it as such. Further, the time of the board is limited – they do not want to waste it, and neither should you.

4) Do not exaggerate your experience or abilities

In the first place, from information in the application or other interviews and sources, the board may know more about you than you think. Secondly, you probably will not get away with it. An experienced board is rather adept at spotting such a situation, so do not take the chance.

5) If you know a board member, do not make a point of it, yet do not hide it

Certainly you are not fooling him, and probably not the other members of the board. Do not try to take advantage of your acquaintanceship – it will probably do you little good.

6) Do not dominate the interview

Let the board do that. They will give you the clues – do not assume that you have to do all the talking. Realize that the board has a number of questions to ask you, and do not try to take up all the interview time by showing off your extensive knowledge of the answer to the first one.

7) Be attentive

You only have 20 minutes or so, and you should keep your attention at its sharpest throughout. When a member is addressing a problem or question to you, give him your undivided attention. Address your reply principally to him, but do not exclude the other board members.

8) Do not interrupt

A board member may be stating a problem for you to analyze. He will ask you a question when the time comes. Let him state the problem, and wait for the question.

9) Make sure you understand the question

Do not try to answer until you are sure what the question is. If it is not clear, restate it in your own words or ask the board member to clarify it for you. However, do not haggle about minor elements.

10) Reply promptly but not hastily

A common entry on oral board rating sheets is "candidate responded readily," or "candidate hesitated in replies." Respond as promptly and quickly as you can, but do not jump to a hasty, ill-considered answer.

11) Do not be peremptory in your answers

A brief answer is proper – but do not fire your answer back. That is a losing game from your point of view. The board member can probably ask questions much faster than you can answer them.

12) Do not try to create the answer you think the board member wants

He is interested in what kind of mind you have and how it works – not in playing games. Furthermore, he can usually spot this practice and will actually grade you down on it.

13) Do not switch sides in your reply merely to agree with a board member

Frequently, a member will take a contrary position merely to draw you out and to see if you are willing and able to defend your point of view. Do not start a debate, yet do not surrender a good position. If a position is worth taking, it is worth defending.

14) Do not be afraid to admit an error in judgment if you are shown to be wrong

The board knows that you are forced to reply without any opportunity for careful consideration. Your answer may be demonstrably wrong. If so, admit it and get on with the interview.

15) Do not dwell at length on your present job

The opening question may relate to your present assignment. Answer the question but do not go into an extended discussion. You are being examined for a *new* job, not your present one. As a matter of fact, try to phrase ALL your answers in terms of the job for which you are being examined.

Basis of Rating

Probably you will forget most of these "do's" and "don'ts" when you walk into the oral interview room. Even remembering them all will not ensure you a passing grade. Perhaps you did not have the qualifications in the first place. But remembering them will help you to put your best foot forward, without treading on the toes of the board members.

Rumor and popular opinion to the contrary notwithstanding, an oral board wants you to make the best appearance possible. They know you are under pressure – but they also want to see how you respond to it as a guide to what your reaction would be under the pressures of the job you seek. They will be influenced by the degree of poise you display, the personal traits you show and the manner in which you respond.

ABOUT THIS BOOK

This book contains tests divided into Examination Sections. Go through each test, answering every question in the margin. We have also attached a sample answer sheet at the back of the book that can be removed and used. At the end of each test look at the answer key and check your answers. On the ones you got wrong, look at the right answer choice and learn. Do not fill in the answers first. Do not memorize the questions and answers, but understand the answer and principles involved. On your test, the questions will likely be different from the samples. Questions are changed and new ones added. If you understand these past questions you should have success with any changes that arise. Tests may consist of several types of questions. We have additional books on each subject should more study be advisable or necessary for you. Finally, the more you study, the better prepared you will be. This book is intended to be the last thing you study before you walk into the examination room. Prior study of relevant texts is also recommended. NLC publishes some of these in our Fundamental Series. Knowledge and good sense are important factors in passing your exam. Good luck also helps. So now study this Passbook, absorb the material contained within and take that knowledge into the examination. Then do your best to pass that exam.

EXAMINATION SECTION

EXAMINATION SECTION
TEST 1

DIRECTIONS: Each question or incomplete statement is followed by several suggested answers or completions. Select the one that BEST answers the question or completes the statement. *PRINT THE LETTER OF THE CORRECT ANSWER IN THE SPACE AT THE RIGHT.*

1. When you select someone to serve as supervisor of your unit during your absence on vacation and at other times, it would generally be BEST to choose the employee who is 1.____

   A. able to move the work along smoothly without friction
   B. on staff longest
   C. liked best by the rest of the staff
   D. able to perform the work of each employee to be supervised

2. Successful supervision of handicapped persons employed in a department depends MOST on providing them with a work place and work climate 2.____

   A. which is safe and accident-free
   B. that requires close and direct supervision by others
   C. that requires the performance of routine, repetitive tasks under a minimum of pressure
   D. where they will be accepted by the other employees

3. Studies have indicated that when employees feel that their work is aimless and unchallenging, the allocation or payment of more money for this type of work is LIKELY to 3.____

   A. contribute little to increased production
   B. bring more status to this work
   C. increase employees' feelings of security
   D. give employees greater motivation

4. An employee's performance has fallen below established minimum standards of quantity and quality. 4.____
   The threat of monetary or other disciplinary action as a device for improving this employee's performance would PROBABLY be acceptable and most effective

   A. only if applied as soon as the performance fell below standard
   B. only after more constructive techniques have failed
   C. at any time provided the employee understands that the punishment will be carried out
   D. at no time

5. A supervisor must, on short notice, ask his staff to work overtime. 5.____
   Of the following, a technique that is MOST likely to win their willing cooperation would be to

   A. explain that occasional overtime is part of the job requirement
   B. explain that they will be doing him a personal favor which he will appreciate very much
   C. explain why the overtime is necessary
   D. promise them that they can take the extra time off in the near future

6. On checking a completed work assignment of an employee, the supervisor finds that the work was not done correctly because the employee had not understood his instructions. Of the following, the BEST way to prevent repetition of this situation next time is for the supervisor to 6.____

   A. ask the employee whether he fully understood the instructions and tell him to ask questions in the future whenever anything is unclear
   B. ask the employee to repeat the instructions given and test his understanding with several key questions
   C. give the instructions a second time, emphasizing the more complicated aspects of the job
   D. give work instructions in writing

7. If, as a supervisor, you find yourself pressured for time to handle all of your job responsibilities, the one of the following tasks which it would be MOST appropriate for you to delegate to a subordinate is 7.____

   A. attending a staff conference of unit supervisors to discuss the implementation of a new departmental policy
   B. making staff work assignments
   C. interviewing a new employee
   D. checking work of certain employees for accuracy

8. Suppose you are unavoidably late for work one morning. When you arrive at 10 o'clock, you find there are several matters demanding your attention. Which one of the following matters should you handle LAST? 8.____

   A. A visitor who had a 9:30 appointment with you has been waiting to see you since 9 o'clock
   B. An employee on an assignment which should have been completed that morning is absent, and the work will have to be reassigned
   C. Several letters which you dictated at the end of the previous day have been typed and are on your desk for signature and mailing
   D. Your superior called asking you to get certain information for him when you come in and to call him back

9. Suppose that you have assigned a typist to type a report containing considerable statistical and tabular material and have given her specific instructions as to how this material is to be laid out on each page. When she returns the completed report, you find that it was not prepared according to your instructions, but you may possibly be able to use it the way it was typed. When you question her, she states that she thought her layout was better, but you were unavailable for consultation when she began the work. Of the following, the BEST action for you to take is to 9.____

   A. criticize her for not doing the work according to your instructions
   B. have her retype the report
   C. praise her for her work but tell her she could have waited until she could consult you
   D. praise her for using initiative

10. Of the following, the MOST effective way for a supervisor to correct poor working habits of an employee which result in low and poor quality output is to give the employee 10.____

A. additional training
B. less demanding assignments until his work improves
C. continuous supervision
D. more severe criticism

11. Of the following, the BEST way for a supervisor to teach an employee how to do a new and somewhat complicated job is to 11.____

A. assign him to observe another employee who is already skilled in this work and instruct him to consult this employee if he has any questions
B. explain to him how to do it, then demonstrate how it is done, then observe and correct the employee as he does it, then follow up
C. give him a written, detailed, step-by-step explanation of how to do the job and instruct him to ask questions if anything is unclear when he does the work
D. teach him the easiest part of the job first, then the other parts one at a time, in order of their difficulty, as the employee masters the easier parts

12. After an employee has completed telling his supervisor about a grievance against a co-worker, the supervisor tells the employee that he will take action to remove the cause of the grievance. 12.____
The action of the supervisor was

A. *good* because ill feeling between subordinates interferes with proper performance
B. *poor* because the supervisor should give both employees time to *cool off*
C. *good* because grievances that appear petty to the supervisor are important to subordinates
D. *poor* because the supervisor should tell the employee that he will investigate the matter before he comes to any conclusion

13. During work on an important project, one employee in a secretarial pool turns in several pages of typed copy, one page of which contains several errors. 13.____
Of these four comments which her supervisor might possibly make, which one would be MOST constructive?

A. "You did such a poor job on this; I 'll have to have it done over."
B. "You will have to do better more consistently than this if you want to be in charge of a secretarial pool yourself someday."
C. "How come you made so many mistakes here? Your other pages were all right."
D. "If my boss saw this, he'd be very displeased with you."

14. A supervisor has general supervision over a large, complex project with many employees. The work is subdivided among small units of employees, each with a senior clerk or senior stenographer in charge. At a staff meeting, after all work assignments have been made, the supervisor tells all the employees that they are to take orders only from their immediate supervisor and instructs them to let him know if any one else tries to give them orders. 14.____
This instruction by the supervisor is

A. *good* because it may prevent the issuance of orders by unauthorized persons which would interfere with the accomplishment of the assignment
B. *poor* because employees should be instructed to take up such problems with their immediate supervisor

C. *good* because orders issued by immediate supervisors would be precise and directly related to the tasks of the assignments while those issued by others would not be
D. *poor* because it places upon all employees a responsibility which should not normally be theirs

15. A supervisor who is to direct a team of senior clerks and clerks and senior stenographers and stenographers in a complex project calls them together beforehand to inform them of the tasks each employee will perform on this job. Of the following, the CHIEF value of this action by the supervisor is that each member of this team will be able to 15.____

A. work independently in the absence of the supervisor
B. understand what he will do and how this will fit into the total picture
C. share in the process of decision-making as an equal participant
D. judge how well the plans for this assignment have been made

16. A supervisor who has both younger and older employees under his supervision may sometimes find that employee absenteeism seriously interferes with accomplishment of goals. 16.____
Studies of such employee absenteeism have shown that the absences of employees

A. under 35 years of age are usually unexpected and the absences of employees over 45 years of age are usually unnecessary
B. of all age groups show the same characteristics as to length of absence
C. under 35 years of age are for frequent, short periods while the absences of employees over 45 years of age are less frequent but of longer duration
D. under 35 years of age are for periods of long duration and the absences of employees over 45 years of age are for periods of short duration

17. Suppose you have a long-standing procedure for getting a certain job done by your subordinates that is apparently a good one. Changes in some steps of the procedure are made from time to time to handle special problems that come up. 17.____
For you to review this procedure periodically is desirable MAINLY because

A. the system is working well
B. checking routines periodically is a supervisor's chief responsibility
C. subordinates may be confused as to how the procedure operates as a result of the changes made
D. it is necessary to determine whether the procedure has become outdated or is in need of improvement

18. In conducting an interview, the BEST types of questions with which to begin the interview are those which the person interviewed is ______ to answer. 18.____

A. willing and able
B. willing but unable
C. able to but unwilling
D. unable and unwilling

19. In order to determine accurately a child's age, it is BEST for an interviewer to rely on 19.____

A. the child's grade in school
B. what the mother says
C. birth records
D. a library card

20. In his first interview with a new employee, it would be LEAST appropriate for a unit supervisor to 20.____

    A. find out the employee's preference for the several types of jobs to which he is able to assign him
    B. determine whether the employee will make good promotion material
    C. inform the employee of what his basic job responsibilities will be
    D. inquire about the employee's education and previous employment

21. If an interviewer takes care to phrase his questions carefully and precisely, the result will MOST probably be that 21.____

    A. he will be able to determine whether the person interviewed is being truthful
    B. the free flow of the interview will be lost
    C. he will get the information he wants
    D. he will ask stereotyped questions and narrow the scope of the interview

22. When, during an interview, is the person interviewed LEAST likely to be cautious about what he tells the interviewer? 22.____

    A. Shortly after the beginning when the questions normally suggest pleasant associations to the person interviewed
    B. As long as the interviewer keeps his questions to the point
    C. At the point where the person interviewed gains a clear insight into the area being discussed
    D. When the interview appears formally ended and goodbyes are being said

23. In an interview held for the purpose of getting information from the person interviewed, it is sometimes desirable for the interviewer to repeat the answer he has received to a question. 23.____
    For the interviewer to rephrase such an answer in his own words is good practice MAINLY because it

    A. gives the interviewer time to make up his next question
    B. gives the person interviewed a chance to correct any possible misunderstanding
    C. gives the person interviewed the feeling that the interviewer considers his answer important
    D. prevents the person interviewed from changing his answer

24. There are several methods of formulating questions during an interview. The particular method used should be adapted to the interview problems presented by the person being questioned. 24.____
    Of the following methods of formulating questions during an interview, the ACCEPTABLE one is for the interviewer to ask questions which

    A. incorporate several items in order to allow a cooperative interviewee freedom to organize his statements
    B. are ambiguous in order to foil a distrustful interviewee
    C. suggest the correct answer in order to assist an interviewee who appears confused
    D. would help an otherwise unresponsive interviewee to become more responsive

25. For an interviewer to permit the person being interviewed to read the data the interviewer writes as he records the person's responses on a routine departmental form is 25.____

A. *desirable* because it serves to assure the person interviewed that his responses are being recorded accurately
B. *undesirable* because it prevents the interviewer from clarifying uncertain points by asking additional questions
C. *desirable* because it makes the time that the person interviewed must wait while the answer is written seem shorter
D. *undesirable* because it destroys the confidentiality of the interview

26. Suppose that a stranger enters the office you are in charge of and asks for the address and telephone number of one of your employees. 26.____
Of the following, it would be BEST for you to

A. find out why he needs the information and release it if his reason is a good one
B. explain that you are not permitted to release such information to unauthorized persons
C. give him the information but tell him it must be kept confidential
D. ask him to leave the office immediately

27. A member of the public approaches an employee who is at work at his desk. The employee cannot interrupt his work in order to take care of this person. 27.____
Of the following, the BEST and MOST courteous way of handling this situation is for the employee to

A. avoid looking up from his work until he is finished with what he is doing
B. tell this person that he will not be able to take care of him for quite a while
C. refer the individual to another employee who can take care of him right away
D. chat with the individual while he continues with his work

28. You answer a phone call from a citizen who urgently needs certain information you do not have, but you think you know who may have it. He is angry because he has already been switched to two different offices. 28.____
Of the following, it would be BEST for you to

A. give him the phone number of the person you think may have the information he wants, but explain you are not sure
B. tell him you regret you cannot help him because you are not sure who can give him the information
C. advise him that the best way he can be sure of getting the information he wants is to write a letter to the agency
D. get the phone number where he can be reached and tell him you will try to get the information he wants and will call him back later

29. Persons who have business with an agency often complain about the *red tape* which complicates or slows up what they are trying to accomplish. 29.____
As a supervisor of a unit which deals with the public, the LEAST effective of the following actions which you could take to counteract this feeling on the part of a person who has business with your office is to

A. assure him that your office will make every effort to take care of his matter as fast as possible
B. tell him that because of the volume of work in your agency he must be patient with *red tape*

C. give him a reasonable date by which action on the matter he is concerned about will be completed and tell him to call you if he hasn't heard by then
D. give him an understanding of why the procedures he must comply with are necessary

30. If a receptionist is sorting letters at her desk and a caller appears to make an inquiry, the receptionist should 30.____

A. ask the caller to have a seat and wait
B. speak to the caller while continuing the sorting, looking up occasionally
C. stop what she is doing and give undivided attention to the caller
D. continue with the sorting until a logical break in the work is reached, then answer any inquiries

31. To avoid cutting off parts of letters when using an automatic letter opener, it is BEST to 31.____

A. arrange all of the letters so that the addresses are right side up
B. hold the envelopes up to the light to make sure their contents have not settled to the side that is to be opened
C. strike the envelopes against a table or desk top several times so that the contents of all the envelopes settle to one side
D. check the enclosures periodically to make sure that the machine has not been cutting into them

32. Requests to repair office equipment which appears to be unsafe should be given priority MAINLY because if repairs are delayed 32.____

A. there may be injuries to staff
B. there may be further deterioration of the equipment
C. work flow may be interrupted
D. the cost of repair may increase

33. Of the following types of documents, it is MOST important to retain and file 33.____

A. working drafts of reports that have been submitted in final form
B. copies of letters of good will which conveyed a message that could not be handled by phone
C. interoffice orders for materials which have been received and verified
D. interoffice memoranda regarding the routing of standard forms

34. Of the following, the BEST reason for discarding certain material from office files would be that the 34.____

A. files are crowded
B. material in the files is old
C. material duplicates information obtainable from other sources in the files
D. material is referred to most often by employees in an adjoining office

35. Of the following, the BEST reason for setting up a partitioned work area for the typists in your office is that 35.____

A. an uninterrupted flow of work among the typists will be possible
B. complaints about ventilation and lighting will be reduced
C. the first-line supervisor will have more direct control over the typists
D. the noise of the typewriters will be less disturbing to other workers

36. Of the following, the MAIN factor contributing to the expense of maintaining an office procedure manual would be the 36.____

A. infrequent use of the manual
B. need to revise it regularly
C. cost of looseleaf binders
D. high cost of printing

37. From the viewpoint of use of a typewriter to fill in a form, the MOST important design factor to consider is 37.____

A. standard spacing
B. box headings
C. serial numbering
D. vertical guide lines

38. Out-of-date and seldom used records should be removed PERIODICALLY from the files because 38.____

A. overall responsibility for records will be transferred to the person in charge of the central storage files
B. duplicate copies of every record are not needed
C. valuable filing space will be regained and the time needed to find a current record will be cut down
D. worthwhile suggestions on improving the filing system will result whenever this is done

39. In a certain office, file folders are constantly being removed from the files for use by administrators. At the same time, new material is coming in to be filed in some of these folders. 39.____
Of the following, the BEST way to avoid delays in filing of the new material and to keep track of the removed folders is to

A. keep a sheet listing all folders removed from the file, who has them, and a follow-up date to check on their return; attach to this list new material received for filing
B. put an *out* slip in the place of any file folder removed, telling what folder is missing, date removed, and who has it; file new material received at front of files
C. put a temporary *out* folder in place of the one removed, giving title or subject, date removed, and who has it; put into this temporary folder any new material received
D. keep a list of all folders removed and who has them; forward any new material received for filing while a folder is out to the person who has it

40. Folders labeled *Miscellaneous* should be used in an alphabetic filing system MAINLY to 40.____

A. provide quick access to recent material
B. avoid setting up individual folders for all infrequent correspondents
C. provide temporary storage for less important documents
D. temporarily hold papers which will not fit into already crowded individual folders

41. Suppose that one of the office machines in your unit is badly in need of replacement. Of the following, the MOST important reason for postponing immediate purchase of a new machine would be that 41.____

A. a later model of the machine is expected on the market in a few months
B. the new machine is more expensive than the old machine
C. the operator of the present machine will have to be instructed by the manufacturer in the operation of the new machine
D. the employee operating the old machine is not complaining

42. If the four steps listed below for processing records were given in logical sequence, the one that would be the THIRD step is: 42.____

A. Coding the records, using a chart or classification system
B. Inspecting the records to make sure they have been released for filing
C. Preparing cross-reference sheets or cards
D. Skimming the records to determine filing captions

43. The suggestion that memos or directives which circulate among subordinates be initialed by each employee is a 43.____

A. *poor* one because, with modern copying machines, it should be possible to supply every subordinate with a copy of each message for his personal use
B. *good* one because it relieves the supervisor of blame for the action of subordinates who have read and initialed the messages
C. *poor* one because initialing the memo or directive is no guarantee that the subordinate has read the material
D. *good* one because it can be used as a record by the supervisor to show that his subordinates have received the message and were responsible for reading it

44. Of the following, the MOST important reason for microfilming office records is to 44.____

A. save storage space needed to keep records
B. make it easier to get records when needed
C. speed up the classification of information
D. shorten the time which records must be kept

45. Your office filing cabinets have become so overcrowded that it is difficult to use the files. Of the following, the MOST desirable step for you to take FIRST to relieve this situation would be to 45.____

A. assign your assistant to spend some time each day reviewing the material in the files and to give you his recommendations as to what material may be discarded
B. discard all material which has been in the files more than a given number of years
C. submit a request for additional filing cabinets in your next budget request
D. transfer enough material to the central storage room of your agency to give you the amount of additional filing space needed

46. Of the following, the USUAL order of the subdivisions in a standard published report is: 46.____

A. Table of contents, body of report, index, appendix
B. Index, table of contents, body of report, appendix
C. Index, body of report, table of contents, appendix
D. Table of contents, body of report, appendix, index

47. The BEST type of pictorial illustration to show the approximate percentage breakdown of the titles of employees in a department would be the 47.____

A. flow chart
B. bar graph
C. organization chart
D. line graph

48. You are reviewing a draft, written by one of your subordinates, of a report that is to be distributed to every bureau and division of your department. Which one of the following would be the LEAST desirable characteristic of such a report? 48.___

A. It gives information, explanations, conclusions, and recommendations for which purpose it was written.
B. There is sufficient objective data presented to substantiate the conclusions reached and the recommendations made by the writer.
C. The writing style and opinions of the writer are persuasive enough to win over to its conclusions those who read the report, although little data is given in support.
D. It will be understood easily by the people to whom it will be distributed.

49. According to accepted practice, a business letter is addressed to an organization but marked for the attention of a specific individual whenever the sender wants 49.___

A. only the person to whose attention the letter is sent to read the letter
B. the letter to be opened and taken care of by someone else in the organization of the person for whose attention it is marked is away
C. a reply only from the specific individual
D. to improve the appearance and balance of the letter in cases where the company address is a long one

50. Which one of the following would be an ACCEPTABLE way to end a business letter? 50.___

A. Hoping you will find this information useful, I remain
B. Yours for continuing service
C. I hope this letter gives you the information you need
D. Trusting this gives you the information you desire, I am

KEY (CORRECT ANSWERS)

1. A	11. B	21. C	31. C	41. A
2. D	12. D	22. D	32. A	42. A
3. A	13. C	23. B	33. D	43. D
4. B	14. B	24. D	34. C	44. A
5. C	15. B	25. A	35. D	45. A
6. B	16. C	26. B	36. B	46. D
7. D	17. D	27. C	37. A	47. B
8. C	18. A	28. D	38. C	48. C
9. A	19. C	29. B	39. C	49. B
10. A	20. B	30. C	40. B	50. C

TEST 2

DIRECTIONS: Each question or incomplete statement is followed by several suggested answers or completions. Select the one that BEST answers the question or completes the statement. *PRINT THE LETTER OF THE CORRECT ANSWER IN THE SPACE AT THE RIGHT.*

1. You are replying to a letter from an individual who asks for a pamphlet put out by your agency. The pamphlet is out of print. A new pamphlet with a different title, but dealing with the same subject, is available. 1._____
   Of the following, it would be BEST that your reply indicate that

   A. you cannot send him the pamphlet he requested because it is out of print
   B. the pamphlet he requested is out of print, but he may be able to find it in the public library
   C. the pamphlet he requested is out of print, but you are sending him a copy of your agency's new pamphlet on the same subject
   D. since the pamphlet he requested is out of print, you would advise him to ask his friends or business acquaintances if they have a copy of it

2. An angry citizen sends a letter to your agency claiming that your office sent him the wrong form and complaining about the general inefficiency of city workers. Upon checking, you find that an incorrect form was indeed sent to this person. 2._____
   In reply, you should

   A. admit the error, apologize briefly, and enclose the correct form
   B. send the citizen the correct form with a transmittal letter stating only that the form is enclosed
   C. send him the correct form without any comment
   D. advise the citizen that mistakes happen in every large organization and that you are enclosing the correct form

3. It has been suggested that the language level of a letter of reply written by a government employee be geared no higher than the probable educational level of the person to whom the letter is written. 3._____
   This suggestion is a

   A. *good* one because it is easier for anyone to write letters simply, and this will make for a better reply
   B. *poor* one because it is not possible to judge, from one letter, the exact educational level of the writer
   C. *good* one because it will contribute to the recipient's comprehension of the contents of the letter
   D. *poor* one because the language should be at the simplest possible level so that anyone who reads the letter can understand it

4. Suppose that a large bureau has 187 employees. On a particular day, approximately 14% of these employees are not available for work because of absences due to vacation, illness, or other reasons. Of the remaining employees, 1/7 are assigned to a special project while the balance are assigned to the normal work of the bureau. 4._____
   The number of employees assigned to the normal work of the bureau on that day is

   A. 112 B. 124 C. 138 D. 142

5. Suppose that you are in charge of a typing pool of 8 typists. Two typists type at the rate of 38 words per minute; three type at the rate of 40 words per minute; three type at the rate of 42 words per minute. The average typewritten page consists of 50 lines, 12 words per line. Each employee works from 9 to 5 with one hour off for lunch. The total number of pages typed by this pool in one day is, on the average, CLOSEST to ______ pages. 5.____

   A. 205 B. 225 C. 250 D. 275

6. Suppose that part-time workers are paid $14.40 an hour, prorated to the nearest half hour, with pay guaranteed for a minimum of four hours if services are required for less than four hours. In one operation, part-time workers signed the time sheet as follows: 6.____

Worker	In	Out
A	8:00 A.M.	11:35 A.M.
B	8:30 A.M.	3:20 P.M.
C	7:55 A.M.	11:00 A.M.
D	8:30 A.M.	2:25 P.M.

How much would total payment to these part-time workers amount to for this operation, assuming that those who stayed after 12 Noon were not paid for one hour which they took off for lunch?

   A. $268.80 B. $273.60 C. $284.40 D. $297.60

7. He wanted to *ascertain* the facts before arriving at a conclusion. The word *ascertain* means MOST NEARLY 7.____

   A. disprove B. determine C. convert D. provide

8. Did the supervisor *assent* to her request for annual leave? The word *assent* means MOST NEARLY 8.____

   A. allude B. protest C. agree D. refer

9. The new worker was fearful that the others would *rebuff* her. The word *rebuff* means MOST NEARLY 9.____

   A. ignore B. forget C. copy D. snub

10. The supervisor of that office does not *condone* lateness. The word *condone* means MOST NEARLY 10.____

   A. mind B. excuse C. punish D. remember

11. Each employee was instructed to be as *concise* as possible when preparing a report. The word *concise* means MOST NEARLY 11.____

   A. exact B. sincere C. flexible D. brief

Questions 12-21.

DIRECTIONS: Below are 10 sentences numbered 12 to 21. Some of the sentences contain an error in spelling, word usage, or sentence structure, or punctuation. Some sentences are correct as they stand, although there may be other correct ways of expressing the same thought. All incorrect sentences contain only one error. Mark your answer to each question as follows:

A. if the sentence has an error in spelling
B. if the sentence has an error in punctuation or capitalization
C. if the sentence has an error in word usage or sentence structure
D. if the sentence is correct

12. Because the chairman failed to keep the participants from wandering off into irrelevant discussions, it was impossible to reach a consensus before the meeting was adjourned. 12.____

13. Certain employers have an unwritten rule that any applicant, who is over 55 years of age, is automatically excluded from consideration for any position whatsoever. 13.____

14. If the proposal to build schools in some new apartment buildings were to be accepted by the builders, one of the advantages that could be expected to result would be better communication between teachers and parents of schoolchildren. 14.____

15. In this instance, the manufacturer's violation of the law against deseptive packaging was discernible only to an experienced inspector. 15.____

16. The tenants' anger stemmed from the president's going to Washington to testify without consulting them first. 16.____

17. Did the president of this eminent banking company say; "We intend to hire and train a number of these disad-vantaged youths?" 17.____

18. In addition, today's confidential secretary must be knowledgable in many different areas: for example, she must know modern techniques for making travel arrangements for the executive. 18.____

19. To avoid further disruption of work in the offices, the protesters were forbidden from entering the building unless they had special passes. 19.____

20. A valuable secondary result of our training conferences is the opportunities afforded for management to observe the reactions of the participants. 20.____

21. Of the two proposals submitted by the committee, the first one is the best. 21.____

Questions 22-26.

DIRECTIONS: In Questions 22 through 26, choose the sentence which is BEST from the point of view of English usage suitable for a business letter or report.

22. 22.____
A. It is the opinion of the Commissioners that programs which include the construction of cut-rate municipal garages in the central business district is inadvisable.
B. Having reviewed the material submitted, the program for putting up cut-rate garages in the central business district seemed likely to cause traffic congestion.
C. The Commissioners believe that putting up cut-rate municipal garages in the central business district is inadvisable.
D. Making an effort to facilitate the cleaning of streets in the central business district, the building of cut-rate municipal garages presents the problem that it would encourage more motorists to come into the central city.

23. A. This letter, together with the reports, are to be sent to the principal. 23.____
B. The reports, together with this letter, is to be sent to the principal.
C. The reports and this letter is to be sent to the principal.
D. This letter, together with the reports, is to be sent to the principal.

24. A. Each employee has to decide for themselves whether to take the examination. 24.____
B. Each of the employees has to decide for himself whether to take the examination.
C. Each of the employees has to decide for themselves whether to take the examination.
D. Each of the employees have to decide for himself whether to take the examination.

25. A. The reason a new schedule is being prepared is that there has been a change in priorities. 25.____
B. Because there has been a change in priorities is the reason why a new schedule is being made up.
C. The reason why a new schedule is being made up is because there has been a change in priorities.
D. Because of a change in priorities is the reason why a new schedule is being prepared.

26. A. The changes in procedure had an unfavorable affect upon the output of the unit. 26.____
B. The increased output of the unit was largely due to the affect of the procedural changes.
C. The changes in procedure had the effect of increasing the output of the unit.
D. The increased output of the unit from the procedural changes were the effect.

Questions 27-33.

DIRECTIONS: Questions 27 through 33 are to be answered SOLELY on the basis of the information in the following extract, which is from a report prepared for Department X, which outlines the procedure to be followed in the case of transfers of employees.

Every transfer, regardless of the reason therefor, requires completion of the record of transfer, Form DT 411. To denote consent to the transfer, DT 411 should contain the signatures of the transferee and the personnel officer(s) concerned, except that, in the case of an involuntary transfer, the signatures of the transferee's present and prospective supervisors shall be entered in Boxes 8A and 8B, respectively, since the transferee does not consent. Only a permanent employee may request a transfer; in such cases, the employee's attendance record shall be duly considered with regard to absences, latenesses, and accrued overtime balances. In the case of an inter-district transfer, the employee's attendance record must be included in Section 8A of the transfer request, Form DT 410, by the personnel officer of the district from which the transfer is requested. The personnel officer of the district to which the employee requested transfer may refuse to accept accrued overtime balances in excess of ten days.

An employee on probation shall be eligible for transfer. If such employee is involuntarily transferred, he shall be credited for the period of time already served on probation. However, if such transfer is voluntary, the employee shall be required to serve the entire period of his probation in the new position. An employee who has occurred a disability which prevents him from performing his normal duties may be transferred during the period of such disability to other appropriate duties. A disability transfer requires the completion of either Form DT414 if the disability is job-connected, or Form DT 415 if it is not a job-connected disability. In either case, the personnel officer of the district from which the transfer is made signs in Box 6A of the first two copies and the personnel officer of the district to which the transfer is made signs in Box 6B of the last two copies; or, in the case of an intra-district disability transfer, the personnel officer must sign in Box 6A of the first two copies and Box 6B of the last two copies

27. When a personnel officer consents to an employee's request for transfer from his district, this procedure requires that the personnel officer sign Form(s) 27.____

    A. DT 411
    B. DT 410 and DT 411
    C. DT 411 and either Form DT 414 or DT 415
    D. DT 410 and DT 411, and either Form DT 414 or DT 415

28. With respect to the time record of an employee transferred against his wishes during his probationary period, this procedure requires that 28.____

    A. he serve the entire period of his probation in his present office
    B. he lose his accrued overtime balance
    C. his attendance record be considered with regard to absences and latenesses
    D. he be given credit for the period of time he has already served on probation

29. Assume you are a supervisor and an employee must be transferred into your office against his wishes. 29.____
    According to this procedure, the box you must sign on the record of transfer is

    A. 6A B. 8A C. 6B D. 8B

30. Under this procedure, in the case of a disability transfer, when must Box 6A on Forms DT 414 and DT 415 be signed by the personnel officer of the district to which the transfer is being made? 30.____

    A. In all cases when either Form DT 414 or Form DT 415 is used
    B. In all cases when Form DT 414 is used and only under certain circumstances when Form DT 415 is used
    C. In all cases when Form DT 415 is used and only under certain circumstances when Form DT 414 is used
    D. Only under certain circumstances when either Form DT 414 or Form DT 415 is used

31. From the above passage, it may be inferred MOST correctly that the number of copies of Form DT 414 is 31.____

    A. no more than 2
    B. at least 3
    C. at least 5
    D. more than the number of copies of Form DT 415

32. A change in punctuation and capitalization only which would change one sentence into two and possibly contribute to somewhat greater ease of reading of this report extract would be MOST appropriate in the ______ sentence, ______ paragraph. 32.____

A. 2nd; 1st
B. 3rd; 1st
C. next to the last; 2nd
D. 2nd; 2nd

33. In the second paragraph, a word that is INCORRECTLY used is ______ in the ______ sentence. 33.____

A. *shall;* 1st
B. *voluntary;* 3rd
C. *occurred;* 4th
D. *intra-district;* last

Questions 34-38.

DIRECTIONS: Questions 34 through 38 are to be answered SOLELY on the basis of the information contained in the following passage.

Positive discipline minimizes the amount of personal supervision required and aids in the maintenance of standards. When a new employee has been properly introduced and carefully instructed, when he has come to know the supervisor and has confidence in the supervisor's ability to take care of him, when he willingly cooperates with the supervisor, that employee has been under positive discipline and can be put on his own to produce the quantity and quality of work desired. Negative discipline, the fear of transfer to a less desirable location, for example, to a limited extent may restrain certain individuals from overt violation of rules and regulations governing attendance and conduct which in governmental agencies are usually on at least an agency-wide basis. Negative discipline may prompt employees to perform according to certain rules to avoid a penalty such as, for example, docking for tardiness.

34. According to the above passage, it is reasonable to assume that in the area of discipline, the first-line supervisor in a governmental agency has GREATER scope for action in 34.____

A. *positive* discipline because negative discipline is largely taken care of by agency rules and regulations
B. *negative* discipline because rules and procedures are already fixed and the supervisor can rely on them
C. *positive* discipline because the supervisor is in a position to recommend transfers
D. *negative* discipline because positive discipline is reserved for people on a higher supervisory level

35. In order to maintain positive discipline of employees under his supervision, it is MOST important for a supervisor to 35.____

A. assure each employee that he has nothing to worry about
B. insist at the outset on complete cooperation from employees
C. be sure that each employee is well trained in his job
D. inform new employees of the penalties for not meeting standards

36. According to the above passage, a feature of negative discipline is that it 36.____

A. may lower employee morale
B. may restrain employees from disobeying the rules
C. censures equal treatment of employees
D. tends to create standards for quality of work

37. A REASONABLE conclusion based on the above passage is that positive discipline benefits a supervisor because 37.____

A. he can turn over orientation and supervision of a new employee to one of his subordinates
B. subordinates learn to cooperate with one another when working on an assignment
C. it is easier to administer
D. it cuts down, in the long run, on the amount of time the supervisor needs to spend on direct supervision

38. Based on the above passage, it is REASONABLE to assume that an important difference between positive discipline and negative discipline is that positive discipline 38.____

A. is concerned with the quality of work and negative discipline with the quantity of work
B. leads to a more desirable basis for motivation of the employee
C. is more likely to be concerned with agency rules and regulations
D. uses fear while negative discipline uses penalties to prod employees to adequate performance

Questions 39-50.

DIRECTIONS: Questions 39 through 50 are to be answered on the basis of the information given in the graph and chart below.

8 (#2)

ENROLLMENT IN POSTGRADUATE STUDIES

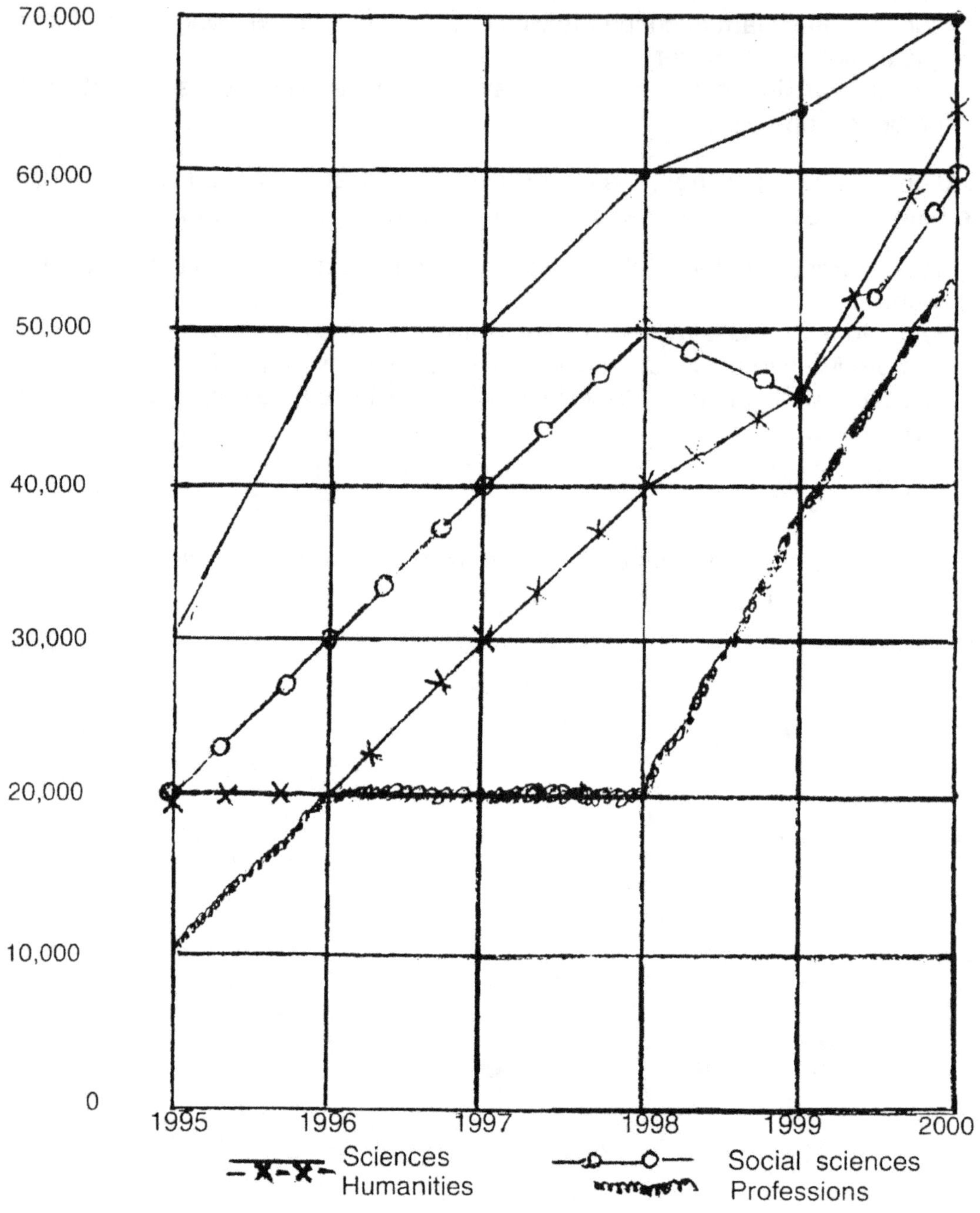

ENROLLMENT IN POSTGRADUATE STUDIES

Fields	Subdivisions	1999	2000
Sciences	Math	10,000	12,000
	Physical science	22,000	24,000
	Behavioral science	32,000	35,000
Humanities	Literature	26,000	34,000
	Philosophy	6,000	8,000
	Religion	4,000	6,000
	Arts	10,000	16,000
Social sciences	History	36,000	46,000
	Sociology	8,000	14.000
Professions	Law	2,000	2,000
	Medicine	6,000	8,000
	Business	30,000	44,000

39. The number of students enrolled in the social sciences and in the humanities was the same in _______ and _______. 39.____

A. 1997; 1999
B. 1995; 1999
C. 1999; 2000
D. 1996; 1999

40. A comparison of the enrollment of students in the various postgraduate studies shows that in every year from 1995 through 2000, there were more students enrolled in the _______ than in the _______. 40.____

A. professions; sciences
B. humanities; professions
C. social sciences; professions
D. humanities; sciences

41. The number of students enrolled in the humanities was GREATER than the number of students enrolled in the professions by the same amount in _______ of the years. 41.____

A. two
B. three
C. four
D. five

42. The one field of postgraduate study to show a decrease in enrollment in one year compared to the year immediately preceding is 42.____

A. humanities
B. sciences
C. professions
D. social sciences

43. If the proportion of arts students to all humanities students was the same in 1997 as in 2000, then the number of arts students in 1997 was 43.____

A. 7,500
B. 13,000
C. 15,000
D. 5,000

44. In which field of postgraduate study did enrollment INCREASE by 20 percent from 1997 to 1998? 44.____

A. Humanities
B. Professions
C. Sciences
D. Social sciences

45. The GREATEST increase in overall enrollment took place between 45.____

A. 1995 and 1996
B. 1997 and 1998
C. 1998 and 1999
D. 1999 and 2000

46. Between 1997 and 2000, the combined enrollment of the sciences and social sciences increased by 46.____

A. 40,000 B. 48,000 C. 50,000 D. 54,000

47. If the enrollment in the social sciences had decreased from 1999 to 2000 at the same rate as from 1998 to 1999, then the social science enrollment in 2000 would have differed from the humanities enrollment in 2000 *MOST* NEARLY by 47.____

A. 6,000 B. 8,000 C. 12,000 D. 22,000

48. In the humanities, the GREATEST percentage increase in enrollment from 1999 to 2000 was in 48.____

A. literature B. philosophy
C. religion D. arts

49. If the proportion of behavioral science students to the total number of students in the sciences was the same in 1996 as in 1999, then the increase in behavioral science enrollment from 1996 to 2000 was 49.____

A. 5,000 B. 7,000 C. 10,000 D. 14,000

50. If enrollment in the professions increased at the same rate from 2000 to 2001 as from 1999 to 2000, the enrollment in the professions in 2001 would be MOST NEARLY 50.____

A. 85,000 B. 75,000 C. 60,000 D. 55,000

KEY (CORRECT ANSWERS)

1. C	11. D	21. C	31. B	41. B
2. A	12. C	22. C	32. B	42. D
3. C	13. B	23. D	33. C	43. A
4. C	14. D	24. B	34. A	44. C
5. B	15. A	25. A	35. C	45. D
6. B	16. D	26. C	36. B	46. A
7. B	17. B	27. A	37. D	47. D
8. C	18. A	28. D	38. B	48. D
9. D	19. C	29. D	39. B	49. C
10. B	20. D	30. D	40. C	50. B

EXAMINATION SECTION
TEST 1

DIRECTIONS: Each question or incomplete statement is followed by several suggested answers or completions. Select the one that BEST answers the question or completes the statement. *PRINT THE LETTER OF THE CORRECT ANSWER IN THE SPACE AT THE RIGHT.*

1. You have recently been assigned to a new office and are expected to supervise six clerks. 1.____
All of the following would be good introductory steps to take EXCEPT

   A. giving a clear presentation of yourself to the clerks, including a short summary of your recent work experience
   B. initiating informal discussions with each clerk concerning his work
   C. making a general survey of all the functions which each clerk has been performing
   D. making a list of the duties each clerk is required to perform and giving it to the clerk

2. Your supervisor has advised you that a specific aspect of a job is being done incorrectly and you acknowledge the mistake. 2.____
Of the following, the MOST efficient way of dealing with this situation is to

   A. call a meeting of the clerks who are performing this particular function and explain the correct method
   B. assume the blame and correct the errors as they are given to you
   C. speak with each clerk individually and carefully show each one the proper method
   D. distribute a set of written instructions covering all clerical procedures to the employees doing that particular job

3. A new department regulation calls for a change in a particular method of processing new applications. Two clerks have complained to you that the new method is more time-consuming, and they prefer to do it the original way. 3.____
Of the following, what is the MOST advisable thing to do?

   A. Discuss the situation with them and attempt to determine whether they are utilizing the method properly.
   B. Discuss the advantages of both methods with them and let them use the one that is more practical.
   C. Firmly instruct the clerks to proceed with the new method since it is not up to them to refute department policy.
   D. Tell them to survey the opinions of the other clerks on this matter and inform you of the results.

4. A member of the clerical staff has recently begun reporting late for work rather regularly. On each occasion, the individual presented an excuse, but the latenesses continue. 4.____
Of the following, the MOST advisable action for her supervisor to take is to

   A. have a staff meeting and stress the importance of being on time for work, without singling out the specific individual
   B. put a notice on the departmental office bulletin board, specifying and stressing that lateness can not be tolerated

C. talk privately with the individual to determine whether theré are any unusual circumstances that might be causing the lateness
D. send the individual a memorandum clearly indicating that continual lateness will result in disciplinary action

5. Assume that, as the supervisor of a unit, you have been asked to prepare a vacation schedule for your subordinate employees. The employees have had different lengths of service. Some of them have already submitted requests for certain weeks. Of the following, which factor would be LEAST important in setting up this schedule? 5.____

A. Your opinion of each employee's past work performance
B. Each employee's preference for a vacation period
C. The amount of work the unit is expected to accomplish during the vacation period
D. The number of employees who have requested to go on vacation at the same time

6. Your superior finds that he must leave the office one day before he has had time to check and sign the day's correspondence. He asks you to proofread the letters, have corrections made where necessary, and then sign his name. You have never signed his name before. Of the following, the BEST thing for you to do is to 6.____

A. sign your superior's name in full, making it look as much like his handwriting as possible
B. sign your superior's name and your own name in full as proof that you signed for him
C. sign your superior's name in full and add your initials to show that the signature is not his own
D. politely refuse to sign his name because it is forgery

7. The head of your office sometimes makes handwritten notations on original letters which he receives and requests that you mail the letters back to the sender. Of the following, the BEST action for you to take FIRST is to 7.____

A. request that this practice be stopped because it does not provide for a record in the files
B. request that this practice be stopped because it is not the customary way to respond to letters
C. photocopy the letters so that there are copies for the file and then send the letters out
D. ask the head of your office if he wants you to keep any record of the letters

8. The main function of most agency administrative offices is *information management*. Information that is received by an administrative office may be classified as active (information which requires the recipient to take some action) or passive (information which does not require action). Which one of the following items received must clearly be treated as ACTIVE information? A(n) 8.____

A. confirmation of payment
B. press release concerning an agency event
C. advertisement for a new restaurant opening near the agency
D. request for a student transcript

9. Which of the following statements about the use of the photocopy process is CORRECT? 9.____

   A. It is difficult to use.
   B. It can be used to reproduce color.
   C. It does not print well on colored paper.
   D. Once source documents have been used, they cannot be used again.

10. In order to get the BEST estimate of how long a repetitive office procedure should take, a supervisor should find out how 10.____

   A. long it takes her best worker to do the procedure once on a typical day
   B. long it takes her best and worst workers to do the procedure once on a typical day
   C. much time her best worker spends on the procedure during a typical week and the total number of times the worker executes the procedure during the same week
   D. much time all her subordinates spend on the procedure during a typical week and the total number of times the procedure was executed during the same week by all employees

11. Of the following, the MOST suitable and appropriate way to make 250 copies of a particular form is to 11.____

   A. print all 250 copies on the office computer
   B. delegate the work to someone else
   C. reproduce it on a photocopying machine
   D. use an offset printing process

Questions 12-18.

DIRECTIONS: Questions 12 through 18 are to be answered on the basis of the extracts shown below from Federal withholding tables. These tables indicate the amounts which must be withheld from the employee's salary by his employer for Federal income tax and for social security. They are based on weekly earnings.

INCOME TAX WITHHOLDING TABLE

The wages are -		And the number of withholding exemptions claimed is-					
At least	But less than	0	1	2	3	4	5
		The amount of income tax to be withheld shall be -					
$200	$205	$14.10	$11.80	$ 9.50	$ 7.20	$ 4.90	$2.80
205	210	14.90	12.60	10.30	8.00	5.70	3.50
210	215	15.70	13.40	11.10	8.80	6.50	4.20
215	220	16.50	14.20	11.90	9.60	7.30	5.00
220	225	17.30	15.00	12.70	10.40	8.10	5.80
225	230	18.10	15.80	13.50	11.20	8.90	6.60
230	235	18.90	16.60	14.30	12.00	9.70	7.40
235	240	19.70	17.40	15.10	12.80	10.50	8.20
240	245	20.50	18.20	15.90	13.60	11.30	9.00
245	250	21.30	19.00	16.70	14.40	12.10	9.80

SOCIAL SECURITY EMPLOYEE TAX TABLE

Wages		Tax to be withheld	Wages		Tax to be withheld
At least	But less than		At least	But less than	
$202.79	$202.99	$15.35	$229.72	$229.91	$16.75
202.99	203.18	15.36	229.91	230.10	16.76
203.18	203.37	15.37	230.10	230.29	16.77
203.37	203.56	15.38	230.29	230.49	16.78
203.56	203.75	15.39	230.49	230.68	16.79
203.75	203.95	15.40	230.68	230.87	16.80
203.95	204.14	15.41	230.87	231.06	16.81
204.14	204.33	15.42	231.06	231.25	16.82
204.33	204.52	15.43	231.25	231.45	16.83
204.52	204.72	15.44	231.45	231.64	16.84

Wages		Tax to be withheld	Wages		Tax to be withheld
At least	But less than		At least	But less than	
$222.02	$222.22	$16.35	$234.52	$234.72	$17.00
222.22	222.41	16.36	234.72	234.91	17.01
222.41	222.60	16.37	234.91	235.10	17.02
222.60	222.79	16.38	235.10	235.29	17.03
222.79	222.99	16.39	235.29	235.49	17.04
222.99	223.18	16.40	235.49	235.68	17.05
223.18	223.37	16.41	235.68	235.87	17.06
223.37	223.56	16.42	235.87	236.06	17.07
223.56	223.75	16.43	236.06	236.25	17.08
223.75	223.95	16.44	236.25	236.45	17.09

12. Dave Andes has wages of $242.75 for one week. He has claimed three withholding exemptions. 12.____
What is the Federal income tax which should be withheld?

A. $13.60 B. $15.90 C. $18.20 D. $20.50

13. Mary Hodes has wages of $229.95 for one week. 13.____
What is the Social Security tax which should be withheld?

A. $16.75 B. $16.76 C. $16.77 D. $16.78

14. Joe Jones had wages of $235.63 for one week. He has claimed two withholding exemptions. 14.____
What is the Federal income tax which should be withheld?

A. $12.80 B. $14.30 C. $15.10 D. $17.40

15. Tom Stein had wages of $203.95 for one week. What is the Social Security tax which should be withheld? 15.____

A. $15.40 B. $15.41 C. $16.05 D. $16.06

16. Robert Helman had wages of $222.80 for one week. He has claimed one withholding exemption. 16.____
If only Federal income tax and Social Security tax were deducted from his earnings for the same week, how much *take-home* pay should he have for the week?

A. $191.41 B. $193.96 C. $194.12 D. $195.65

17. Audrey Stein has wages of $203.00 for one week. She claimed no withholding exemptions. 17.____
If only Federal income tax and Social Security tax were deducted from her earnings for the same week, how much *take-home* pay should she have for the week?

A. $171.84 B. $172.34 C. $173.54 D. $175.84

18. Anthony Covallo, who worked 28 hours in the past week, has a regular hourly rate of $7.25 per hour and earns a premium of time and a half for hours over 40. He has claimed four withholding exemptions. 18.____
After Social Security tax and Federal income tax are deducted from his wages for the past week, how much pay does he have left?

A. $180.98 B. $181.13 C. $182.29 D. $182.74

19. In judging the adequacy of a standard office form, which of the following is LEAST important? 19.____
_______ of the form.

A. Date B. Legibility C. Size D. Design

20. Clear and accurate telephone messages should be taken for employees who are out of the office. 20.____
Which of the following is of LEAST importance when taking a telephone message?

A. Name of the person called
B. Name of the caller

C. Details of the message
D. Time of the call

21. Suppose that all office supplies are kept in a centrally located cabinet in the office. Of the following, which is usually the BEST policy to adhere to for distribution of supplies? 21.____

A. Permit employees to stock up on all supplies to avoid frequent trips to the cabinet.
B. Assign one employee to be in charge of distributing all supplies to other employees at frequent intervals.
C. Inform employees that supplies should be taken in large quantities and only when needed.
D. Keep cabinet closed and instruct employees that they must check with you before taking supplies.

Questions 22-25.

DIRECTIONS: Questions 22 through 25 are to be answered SOLELY on the basis of the following passage.

Use of the systems and procedures approach to office management is revolutionizing the supervision of office work. This approach views an enterprise as an entity which seeks to fulfill definite objectives. Systems and procedures help to organize repetitive work into a routine, thus reducing the amount of decision-making required for its accomplishment. As a result, employees are guided in their efforts and perform only necessary work. Supervisors are relieved of any details of execution and are free to attend to more important work. Establishing work guides which require that identical tasks be performed the same way each, time permits standardization of forms, machine operations, work methods, and controls. This approach also reduces the probability of errors. Any error committed is usually discovered quickly because the incorrect work does not meet the requirement of the work guides. Errors are also reduced through work specialization which allows each employee to become thoroughly proficient in a particular type of work. Such proficiency also tends to improve the morale of the employees.

22. Of the following, which one BEST expresses the main theme of the above passage? The 22.____

A. advantages and disadvantages of the systems and procedures approach to office management
B. effectiveness of the systems and procedures approach to office management in developing skills
C. systems and procedures approach to office management as it relates to office costs
D. advantages of the systems and procedures approach to office management for supervisors and office workers

23. Work guides are LEAST likely to be used when 23.____

A. standardized forms are used
B. a particular office task is distinct and different from all others
C. identical tasks are to be performed in identical ways
D. similar work methods are expected from each employee

24. According to the above passage, when an employee makes a work error, it USUALLY 24.____

A. is quickly corrected by the supervisor
B. necessitates a change in the work guides
C. can be detected quickly if work guides are in use
D. increases the probability of further errors by that employee

25. The above passage states that the accuracy of an employee's work is INCREASED by 25.____

A. using the work specialization approach
B. employing a probability sample
C. requiring him to shift at one time into different types of tasks
D. having his supervisor check each detail of work execution

KEY (CORRECT ANSWERS)

1. D
2. A
3. A
4. C
5. A
6. C
7. D
8. D
9. B
10. D
11. C
12. A
13. B
14. C
15. B
16. A
17. C
18. D
19. A
20. D
21. B
22. D
23. B
24. C
25. A

TEST 2

DIRECTIONS: Each question or incomplete statement is followed by several suggested answers or completions. Select the one that BEST answers the question or completes the statement. *PRINT THE LETTER OF THE CORRECT ANSWER IN THE SPACE AT THE RIGHT.*

1. A certain supervisor often holds group meetings with subordinates to discuss the goals of the unit and manpower requirements for meeting objectives. 1.____
   For the supervisor to hold such meetings is a

   A. *good* practice because it will aid both the supervisor and subordinates in planning and completing the unit's work
   B. *good* practice because it will prevent future problems from interfering with the unit's objectives
   C. *poor* practice because the supervisor has the sole responsibility for meeting objectives and should make manpower decisions without any advice
   D. *poor* practice because the subordinates will be allowed to set their own work quotas

2. Assume that you are a supervisor who has been asked to evaluate the work of a clerk who was transferred to your unit about six months ago. 2.____
   Which one of the following, by itself, provides the BEST basis for making such an evaluation?

   A. Ask the clerk's former supervisor about the employee's previous work.
   B. Ask the clerk's co-workers for their opinions of the employee's work.
   C. Evaluate the quantity and quality of the employee's work over the six-month period.
   D. Observe the employee's performance from time to time during the next week and base your evaluation on these observations.

3. Which of the following would be the MOST desirable way for a supervisor to help improve the job performance of a particular subordinate? 3.____

   A. Criticize the employee's performance in front of other employees.
   B. Privately warn the employee that failure to meet work standards may lead to dismissal.
   C. Hold a meeting with this employee and other subordinates in which the need to improve the unit's performance is stressed.
   D. Meet privately with the employee and discuss both positive and negative aspects of the employee's work

4. Suppose that your office has a limited supply of a pamphlet which people may read in your office when they seek certain information, but another office in your building is supposed to have a large supply available for distribution to the public. 4.____
   Which of the following would be the BEST thing for you to do when someone states that he has not been able to obtain one of these pamphlets?

   A. Tell him that he misunderstood the directions that other employees have given him and carefully direct him to the other office.
   B. Ask whether he has visited the other office and requested a copy from them.
   C. Let him take one of your office's copies of the pamphlet and then call the other office and ask why they have run out of copies for distribution.

D. Tell him that your office does its best to keep the public informed but that this might not be true of other offices.

5. On Monday, a clerk made many errors in completing a new daily record form. The supervisor explained the errors and had the clerk correct the form. On Tuesday, the clerk made fewer errors. Because he was very busy, the supervisor did not point out the errors to the clerk but corrected the errors himself. On Wednesday, the clerk made the same number of errors as on Tuesday. The supervisor reprimanded the clerk for making so many errors. 5.____
The supervisor's handling of this situation on Wednesday may be considered poor MAINLY because the

A. clerk was not given enough time to complete each form properly
B. supervisor should not have expected improvement without further training
C. clerk was obviously incapable of completing the form
D. supervisor should have continued to correct the errors himself

Questions 6-8.

DIRECTIONS: Questions 6 through 8 are to be answered SOLELY on the basis of the information contained in the following passage.

When using words like company, association, *council, committee, and board in place of the full official name, the writer should not capitalize these short forms unless he intends them to invoke the full force of the institution's authority. In legal contracts, in minutes, or in formal correspondence where one is speaking formally and officially on behalf of the company, the term "Company" is usually capitalized, but in ordinary usage, where it is not essential to load the short form with this significance, capitalization would be excessive. (Example: The company will have many good openings for graduates this June.)*

The treatment recommended for short forms of place names is essentially the same as that recommended for short forms of organizational names. In general, we capitalize the full form but not the short form. If Park Avenue is referred to in one sentence, then "the avenue" is sufficient in subsequent references. The same is true with words like building, hotel, station, and airport, which are capitalized when part of a proper name (Pan Am Building, Hotel Plaza, Union Station, O'Hare Airport) but are simply lower-cased when replacing these specific names.

6. The above passage states that USUALLY the short forms of names of organizations 6.____

A. and places should not be capitalized
B. and places should be capitalized
C. should not be capitalized, but the short forms of names of places should be capitalized
D. should be capitalized, but the short forms of names of places should not be capitalized

7. The above passage states that in legal contracts, in minutes, and in formal correspondence, the short forms of names of organizations should 7.____

A. usually not be capitalized
B. usually be capitalized
C. usually not be used
D. never be used

8. It can be INFERRED from the above passage that decisions regarding when to capitalize certain words 8.____

   A. should be left to the discretion of the writer
   B. should be based on generally accepted rules
   C. depend on the total number of words capitalized
   D. are of minor importance

9. The Central Terminal and the Gardens Terminal are located on Glover Street. 9.____
In ordinary usage, if this sentence were to be followed by the sentence in the choices below, which form of the sentence would be CORRECT?

   A. Both Terminals are situated on the same street.
   B. Both terminals are situated on the same Street.
   C. Both terminals are situated on the same street.
   D. Both Terminals are situated on the same Street.

10. A stylus is a(n) 10.____

   A. implement for writing containing a cylinder of graphite
   B. implement for writing with ink or a similar fluid
   C. pointed implement used to write
   D. stick of colored wax used for writing

11. As a supervisor, you have the responsibility of teaching new employees the functions and procedures of your office after their orientation by the personnel office. 11.____
Of the following, the BEST way to begin such instruction is to

   A. advise the new employee of the benefits and services available to him, over and above his salary
   B. discuss the negative aspects of the departmental procedures and indicate methods available to overcome them
   C. assist the new employee in understanding the general purpose of the office procedures and how they fit in with the overall operation
   D. give a detailed briefing of the operations of your office, its functions and procedures

12. Assume that you are the supervisor of a clerical unit. One of the duties of the employees in your unit is to conduct a brief interview with persons using the services of your agency for the first time. The purpose of the interview is to get general background information in order to best direct them to the appropriate division. 12.____
A clerk comes to your office and says that a prospective client has just called her some rather unpleasant names, accused her of being nosey and meddlesome, and has stated emphatically that she refuses to talk with an *underling,* meaning the clerk. The young woman is almost in tears. Of the following, what is the FIRST action you should take?

   A. Immediately call the agency's protection officer, have him advise the client of the regulations, and tell her that she will be removed if she is not more polite.
   B. Calm the clerk, introduce yourself to the client, and quietly discuss the agency's services, regulations, and informational needs, and request that she complete the interview with the clerk.

C. Calm the clerk, have her return and firmly advise the client of the agency's rules concerning the need for this first interview.
D. Introduce yourself to the client and advise her that without an apology to the clerk and completion of the interview, she will not be given any service.

13. A recent high school graduate has just been assigned to the unit which you supervise. Which of the following would be the LEAST desirable technique to use with this employee? 13.____

A. At any one time, give the new employee only as much detail about the job as the employee can absorb.
B. Always tell the new employee the correct procedure, then demonstrate how it is accomplished.
C. Assign the employee the same quantity and type of work that the other employees are doing to see if the employee can handle the job.
D. Assume the employee is tense and be prepared to repeat procedures and descriptions.

14. Assume that you supervise a work unit of several employees. Which of the following is LEAST essential in assuring that the goals which you set for the unit are achieved? 14.____

A. Establishing objectives and standards for the staff
B. Providing justification for disciplinary action
C. Measuring performance or progress of individuals against standards
D. Taking corrective action where performance is less than expected

15. One of the clerks you supervise is often reluctant to accept assignments and usually complains about the amount of work expected, although the other clerks with the same assignments and workload seem quite happy.
Of the following, the MOST accurate assumption that you can make about this clerk is that she 15.____

A. will require additional observation and help
B. will eventually have to be discharged or transferred
C. is incompetent
D. is overworked

Questions 16-21.

DIRECTIONS: Questions 16 through 21 are to be answered SOLELY on the basis of the airline timetable and the information appearing on the last page of this test.

Fact Situation:

An administrator wants you to purchase airline tickets for him so that he can attend a meeting being held in Chicago on Monday. He must leave from LaGuardia Airport in New York on Monday morning as late as possible but with arrival in Chicago no later than 9:00 A.M. He wishes to fly coach/economy class both ways. The meeting is due to end at 5:30 P.M., and he wishes to obtain the first plane after 6:45 P.M. going back to LaGuardia Airport. If all these requirements have been met, he would, if possible, also like to fly to and leave from Midway Airport in Chicago and go non-stop both ways.

16. You should obtain a ticket for the administrator from New York to Chicago on flight number 16.____

A. 483 B. 201 C. 277 D. 539

17. You should obtain a ticket for the administrator from Chicago to New York on flight number 17.____

A. 588 B. 692 C. 268 D. 334

18. The administrator decides to take limousines to and from both airports. 18.____
If the limousine charge in Chicago is $52.50. and there is no reduced rate for a round-trip flight, what is the cost of the administrator's round-trip air fare PLUS limousine service?

A. $827.50 B. $931.00 C. $963.00 D. $967.00

19. The administrator asked you whether he would be able to get breakfast on his flight to Chicago or whether he should go to the airport early and eat there before boarding the plane. He prefers to eat on the plane. 19.____
Of the following, the BEST reply to make is:

A. I will have to telephone the airport to find out
B. You should eat at the airport
C. A meal is served on the plane
D. Only certain passengers get a meal on the plane

20. Of the following requests of the administrator concerning his travel arrangements, which one is IMPOSSIBLE to meet? 20.____

A. Chicago arrival no later than 9 A.M.
B. New York departure from LaGuardia Airport
C. Non-stop flights both ways
D. Chicago departure from Midway Airport

21. Suppose that it is necessary to take a first-class seat on the trip to Chicago although you have no problem reserving a coach/economy seat on the return trip. 21.____
If there is no reduction in fare for round-trip flights, how much MORE will this trip cost than round-trip coach/ economy?

A. $209 B. $236 C. $318 D. $636

22. Ms. X, a clerk under your supervision, has been working in the unit for a few weeks. Some of the other employees have complained to you that Ms. X has an annoying habit of constantly tapping her feet on the floor and it disturbs their work. 22.____
The BEST thing for you to do is to

A. ignore the complaints because the employees should be concerned only with their own habits
B. speak with Ms. X privately and discuss the situation with her
C. make a general announcement that employees should control their nervous habits
D. observe Ms. X for a few weeks to see if the employees are correct, and then take action

23. Suppose you answer a telephone call from someone who states that he is a friend of one of your co-workers and needs the employee's new address in order to send an invitation. Your co-worker is on vacation but you know her address. Which of the following is the BEST action for you to take? 23.____

A. Give the caller the address but ask the caller not to mention that you are the one who gave it out.
B. Give the caller the address and leave a note for your co-worker stating what you did.
C. Tell the caller you do not know the address but will give the employee's phone number if that will help.
D. Offer to take his name and address and have your co-worker contact him.

24. Assume that you receive a telephone call in which the caller requests information which you know is posted in the office next to yours. You start to tell the caller you will transfer her call to the right office, but she interrupts you and says she has been transferred from office to office and is tired of getting a *run-around*. Of the following, the BEST thing for you to do is to 24.____

A. give the caller the phone number of the office next to yours and quickly end the conversation
B. give her the phone number of the office next to yours and tell her you will try to transfer her call
C. ask her if she wants to hold on while you get the information for her
D. tell the caller that she could have avoided the *run-around* by asking for the right office, and suggest that she come in person

25. Assume that your unit processes confidential forms which are submitted by persons seeking financial assistance. An individual comes to your office, gives you his name, and states that he would like to look over a form which he sent in about a week ago because he believes he omitted some important information. Of the following, the BEST thing for you to do FIRST is to 25.____

A. locate the proper form
B. call the individual's home telephone number to verify his identity
C. ask the individual if he has proof of his identity
D. call the security office

KEY (CORRECT ANSWERS)

1. A
2. C
3. D
4. B
5. B
6. A
7. B
8. B
9. C
10. C
11. C
12. B
13. C
14. B
15. A
16. A
17. D
18. B
19. C
20. D
21. C
22. B
23. D
24. C
25. C

EXAMINATION SECTION
TEST 1

DIRECTIONS: Each question or incomplete statement is followed by several suggested answers or completions. Select the one that BEST answers the question or completes the statement. *PRINT THE LETTER OF THE CORRECT ANSWER IN THE SPACE AT THE RIGHT.*

1. As the supervisor of a staff of clerical employees performing various types of work, you are responsible for the accuracy and efficiency with which their work is performed. Of the following actions you may take to insure the accuracy of their work, the MOST practical one is for you to 1.____

   A. review each operation completed by a staff member before permitting the employee to proceed to the next operation
   B. keep a record of every error made by an employee and use this record to determine whether a careless employee should be transferred or discharged
   C. assign work in such a way that every operation is performed independently by two employees
   D. determine what errors are likely to occur and set up safeguards to prevent the occurrence of these errors

2. Assume that you are the supervisor of a small clerical unit. One of your subordinates has violated a staff regulation by failing to inform you that he will be absent on a certain day. Of the following, the MOST appropriate action for you to take first is to 2.____

   A. discuss this matter with your immediate superior
   B. find out the reason for his failure to obey this staff regulation
   C. determine what disciplinary action other supervisors have taken in similar cases
   D. take no action if his absence did not interfere with the work of the unit; reprimand him if it did

3. A newly appointed clerk is assigned to a unit of an agency at a time when the supervisor of the unit is very busy and has little time to devote to instructing the new employee in the work he is to perform. Of the following, the MOST appropriate method of training this employee is for the supervisor to 3.____

   A. instruct the new employee to observe several experienced clerks at work and question them regarding any aspect of the work he does not understand
   B. delegate the job of training this employee to an employee in the unit who is qualified to instruct him
   C. assign the new employee a simple task and inform him that more complex and varied duties will be given him when the supervisor is less busy
   D. have the employee spend his time reading the agency's annual reports and the laws, rules, and regulations governing its work

4. As a supervisor, you may find it necessary to consult with your superior before taking action on some matters. Of the following, the action for which it is MOST important that you obtain the prior approval of your superior is one that involves 4.____

A. assuming additional functions for your unit
B. rotating assignments among your staff members
C. initiating regular meetings of your staff
D. assigning certain members of your staff to work overtime on an emergency job

5. Suppose that a clerk who is employed in a unit under your supervision performs his work quickly but carelessly. He is about to be transferred to another unit in your department. The chief of this other unit asks you for your opinion of this employee's work habits. Of the following, the MOST appropriate reply for you to make is to 5.____

A. point out this employee's good qualities only since he may correct his bad qualities after his transfer is effected
B. say nothing good or bad about this employee, thus permitting him to start his new assignment with a clean slate
C. inform the unit chief that this clerk performed his work speedily but was careless
D. emphasize this employee's good points and minimize his bad points

6. When subordinates request his advice in solving problems encountered in their work, a certain bureau chief occasionally answers the request by first asking the subordinate what he thinks should be done. This action by the bureau chief is, on the whole, 6.____

A. *desirable* because it stimulates subordinates to give more thought to the solution of problems encountered
B. *undesirable* because it discourages subordinates from asking questions
C. *desirable* because it discourages subordinates from asking questions
D. *undesirable* because it undermines the confidence of subordinates in the ability of their supervisor

7. Of the following factors that may be considered by a unit head in dealing with the tardy subordinate, the one which should be given LEAST consideration is the 7.____

A. frequency with which the employee is tardy
B. effect of the employee's tardiness upon the work of other employees
C. willingness of the employee to work overtime when necessary
D. cause of the employee's tardiness

8. Of the following, the action that is likely to contribute MOST to the prestige of a supervisor is for him to 8.____

A. expect all his subordinates to perform with equal efficiency any tasks assigned to them
B. observe the same rules of conduct that he expects his subordinates to observe
C. seek their advice on his personal problems and offer them his advice on their personal problems
D. be always frank and outspoken to his subordinates in pointing out their faults

9. Although an employee under your supervision frequently protests when receiving a monotonous assignment, he nevertheless performs the assigned task efficiently. His protests, however, disturb the other employees and interfere with their work. Of the following actions you may take in handling this employee, the MOST desirable one is for you to 9.____

A. point out to him the effect of his conduct on the staff's work and request his cooperation in accepting such assignments
B. arrange to issue such assignments to him when the other members of his staff are not present
C. inform him that you will request his transfer to another unit unless he puts a halt to his unjustifiable protests
D. ask other members of the staff to tell him that he is disturbing them by his protests

10. Assume that you are the supervisor of a small clerical unit which tabulates data prepared by another unit. One of your employees calls your attention to what appears to be an erroneous figure. 10.____
Of the following, the MOST acceptable advice for you to give this employee is to tell him to

A. omit the figure containing the apparent error and continue with the tabulation
B. make whatever change in the erroneous figure that appears warranted and notify the supervisor of the unit which prepared the data that errors are being made by his staff
C. accept the questionable figure as correct and continue with the tabulation since there is no certainty that an error has been made
D. ask the supervisor of the unit that prepared the data to have the questionable figure checked for accuracy and corrected if it is erroneous

11. A clerk in an agency informs Mr. Brown, an applicant for a license issued by the agency, that the application filed by him was denied because he lacks a year and six months of required experience. Shortly after the applicant leaves the agency's office, the clerk realizes that Mr. Brown lacks only six months of required experience rather than a year and six months. 11.____
Of the following, the MOST desirable procedure to be followed in connection with this matter is that

A. a printed copy of the requirements should be sent to Mr. Brown
B. a letter explaining and correcting the error should be sent to Mr. Brown
C. no action should be taken because Mr. Brown is not qualified at the present time for the license
D. a report of this matter should be prepared and attached to Mr. Brown's application for reference if Mr. Brown should file another application

12. Mr. Stone, who has been recently placed in charge of a clerical unit staffed with ten employees, plans to institute several radical changes in the procedures of his unit. 12.____
Of the following actions he may take before adopting any of the revisions, the MOST desirable one is for Mr. Stone to

A. distribute to each staff member a memorandum describing the revised procedures and requesting the staff's cooperation in giving the revised procedures a fair trial
B. issue to each staff member a memorandum describing the proposed changes and inviting him to submit his written criticism of these proposed changes
C. issue to each staff member a memorandum describing the proposed changes and notifying him of the time and date of a staff conference to be held on the merits of the proposed changes
D. discuss the proposed changes with each staff member independently and obtain his opinion of the proposed changes

13. An assignment completed by Frank King is returned to him by his unit supervisor for certain changes. Frank King objects to making these changes. 13.____
Of the following, the MOST appropriate action for the unit supervisor to take first is to

A. permit Frank King to present his arguments against making these changes
B. inform Frank King that he is free to take the matter up with a higher authority
C. reprimand Frank King for objecting and assign another employee to make these changes
D. state briefly that his decision is final and indicate by his manner that further discussion would be useless

14. A properly conducted job analysis will reveal the qualities essential for efficient job performance. 14.____
Of the following, the MOST accurate implication of this statement is that job analysis

A. enables the supervisor to standardize procedures
B. aids the supervisor in fitting the man to the job
C. is helpful to the supervisor in scheduling work
D. assists the supervisor in estimating costs of jobs

15. All of us who are employed by a government agency are, figuratively speaking, living in glass houses. 15.____
Of the following, this quotation MOST nearly means that employees of government agencies are

A. basically secure in their positions
B. more closely supervised than are those in private industry
C. not free to exercise initiative
D. subject to constant surveillance

16. So important to good supervision is effective leadership that some supervisors who are well equipped in this respect have compensated for deficiencies in other supervisory qualities. 16.____
On the basis of this statement, the MOST accurate of the following statements is that

A. supervisory ability is the most valuable attribute a leader can have
B. effective leaders are generally deficient in other supervisory qualities
C. other supervisory qualities may be substituted for leadership ability
D. good leaders may make good supervisors even though lacking in other supervisory qualities

17. The improvement in skill and the development of proper attitudes are essential factors in the building of correct work habits. 17.____
Of the following, the MOST valid implication of this statement for a supervisor is that

A. the more skilled an employee is, the better will be his attitude toward his work
B. developing proper attitudes in subordinates toward their work is more time-consuming for the supervisor than improving their skill
C. the improvement of a worker's skill is only part of a supervisor's job
D. correct work habits are established in order to either improve the skill of workers or develop in them a proper attitude toward their work

Questions 18-21.

DIRECTIONS: Questions 18 through 21 are based upon the situation described below. Consider the facts given in this situation when answering these questions.

SITUATION: You are the supervisor of a small unit in a large department. In order to assist your staff in handling a peak work load, ten temporary clerks have been hired for a period of two months.

18. Of the following actions you may take before assigning specific tasks to these temporary employees, the MOST appropriate action is for you to 18.____

    A. designate one of their number as your supervisory assistant
    B. find out what clerical experience and training each one has had
    C. ask each member of this group to indicate the type of work he prefers to do
    D. escort this group throughout the department, introducing each temporary employee to all the unit heads in the department

19. The ten temporary employees have been grouped into two teams of five employees each, and the two teams have been given different assignments. After working with his group for several days, an employee in one group asks to be transferred to the other group. 19.____
    Of the following reasons for transferring this employee to the other group, the LEAST acceptable one is that

    A. there is a clash in temperament between him and some of the other members of his group
    B. he can perform the work assigned to the other group more efficiently than he can perform the work assigned to his group
    C. the work assigned to the other group is less monotonous than that assigned to his group
    D. the work assigned to his present group compels him to take frequent rest periods because of a physical disability

20. One of the temporary employees informs you that he has a suggestion for improving the method of performing the work assigned to his group. 20.____
    Of the following actions, the MOST desirable one for you to take is to

    A. ignore his suggestion since he knows little about the purpose of the assignment
    B. ask him to try out the suggestion before submitting it to you
    C. have him discuss it with his co-workers before submitting it to you
    D. listen to his suggestion and take appropriate action

21. A temporary clerk who had been decreasing the amount of work he performed and who had also been attempting to induce other temporary clerks to reduce their production was twice cautioned by you to cease these practices. On each occasion, he promised to discontinue these improper practices and to perform his work conscientiously and cooperatively. Soon thereafter, he is detected for the third time attempting to persuade the other temporary clerks to shirk their duties. 21.____
    Of the following, the MOST appropriate action for you to take is to

A. reprimand him for his improper conduct and have him transferred immediately to another unit
B. remind him that he may not be employed again as a temporary clerk if he continues his unethical practices
C. call a meeting of the temporary staff and warn them that anyone whose production falls below average will be discharged
D. report his improper practices to your immediate superior and recommend that this employee's services be terminated

22. As a supervisor in an agency, you receive a letter from the head of a civic organization requesting information which you are not permitted to divulge. 22.____
In preparing your letter of reply, it is MOST desirable that you

A. begin with a pleasant phrase or statement and conclude with a brief statement denying the request
B. limit your reply to a brief statement denying the request
C. place the denial of the request between a pleasant opening phrase or statement and a cordial closing statement
D. begin with a denial of the request and conclude with a pleasant closing statement

23. Of the following, it is LEAST essential for a supervisor, in assigning work to a subordinate, to issue written instructions when the 23.____

A. supervisor will be on hand to check the work
B. instructions are to be passed on to other employees
C. assignment involves many details
D. subordinate is to be held strictly accountable for the work performed

24. The suggestion is made that all the secretaries assigned to the bureau chiefs of a certain agency can be transferred to a newly established central transcribing unit which is to be staffed with stenographers and typists. Of the following, the MOST probable effect of reassigning these secretaries would be that 24.____

A. the quality of the stenographic and typing work performed by the secretaries would deteriorate
B. the bureau chiefs would be burdened with much of the routine work that is now performed by their secretaries
C. typing and stenographic work would be performed less expeditiously and with frequent delays
D. the development of understudies for bureau chiefs would be greatly hampered

25. In a large agency where both men and women are employed as clerks, certain duties may be assigned more appropriately to women than to men. 25.____
Of the following, the assignment that is generally MOST appropriate for a woman clerk is

A. sorting and filing 3x5 index cards
B. issuing supplies from the agency's stockroom to employees presenting requisitions
C. serving at an information desk during the hours from 7:00 P.M. to 11:00 P.M. for a period of two months
D. collecting outgoing mail from the various offices of the agency and delivering incoming mail to these offices

26. A unit supervisor discovers several errors in the work performed by a subordinate. In dealing with this subordinate, it is LEAST desirable for the supervisor to 26.____

   A. give his criticism immediately rather than at a later date
   B. make it clear to the subordinate that he is criticizing the subordinate and not the subordinate's work
   C. praise, when possible, some commendable aspect of the subordinate's work before making the adverse criticism
   D. make sure that his criticism is not overheard by other employees

27. The status of the morale of a staff is usually a good indication of the quality of the leadership displayed by the supervisor of the staff. 27.____
Of the following, the BEST indication of the existence of high morale among a staff is that

   A. the employees are prompt in reporting for work
   B. the staff is always willing to subordinate personal desires to attain group objectives
   C. it is seldom necessary for the staff to work overtime
   D. the subordinates and their superior meet socially after working hours

28. The use of standard practices and procedures in large organizations is often essential in order to insure a smooth, efficient, and controlled flow of work. A strict adherence to standard practices and procedures to the extent that unnecessary delay is created is known, in general, as *red tape*. 28.____
On the basis of this statement, the MOST accurate of the following statements is that

   A. although the use of standard practices and procedures promotes efficiency, it also creates unnecessary delays and *red tape*
   B. in order to insure a smooth, efficient, and controlled plan of work, *red tape* should be eliminated by a strict adherence to standard practices and procedures
   C. *red tape* is a necessary evil which invariably creeps into any large organization which uses standard practices and procedures
   D. *red* tape exists when delay takes place as a result of a too rigid conformity with standard practices and procedures

29. The tasks of government are imposed not only by law but also by public opinion, which at any time may be made into law. Government agencies must, therefore, strive to anticipate and fulfill the needs of the public. 29.____
Of the following, the MOST valid implication of this statement is that the

   A. satisfaction of the needs of the public is one of the obligations of a government agency
   B. law prescribes what tasks government agencies should perform and public opinion determines how these tasks should be performed
   C. tasks imposed by law on a government agency have priority over those imposed by public opinion
   D. functions of a government agency should be carried out in accordance with the letter, rather than the spirit, of the law

30. The manner in which an employee performs on the job rather than his potential ability is the true test of his value to his employer. 30.____
The one of the following which is NOT an implication of the above statement is a(n)

A. employee of great potential ability may be of little or no value to his employer
B. supervisor should observe the manner in which his subordinates perform their work
C. employee's potential ability is of no significance in determining his fitness for a specific job
D. employee should attempt to perform his work to the best of his ability

31. No routine will automatically bring itself into proper relation with changing conditions. Of the following situations, the one which MOST NEARLY exemplifies the truth of this statement is a 31.____

A. change in the rules governing the submission or reports by employees working in the field is found to be impractical and the previous procedure is reinstituted
B. long established method of filing papers in a bureau is found to be inadequate because of changes in the functions of the bureau
C. long established method of distributing orders to the staff is found to work effectively when the size of the staff is considerably increased
D. change in the rules governing hours of attendance at work proves distasteful to many employees

32. Interest is essentially an attitude of continuing attentiveness, found where activity is satisfactorily self-expressive. Whenever work is so circumscribed that the chance for self-expression or development is denied, monotony is present. 32.____
On the basis of this statement, it is MOST accurate to state that

A. tasks which are repetitive in nature do not permit self-expression and, therefore, create monotony
B. interest in one's work is increased by financial and non-financial incentives
C. jobs which are monotonous can be made self-expressive by substituting satisfactory working conditions
D. workers whose tasks afford them no opportunity for self-expression find such tasks to be monotonous

33. The first step in an organizational study is the reading of the basic documents. There is some documentary basis for any governmental organization, outlining the purposes for which it was established, conferring certain powers, and imposing certain limitations on the conferred powers. This statement indicates that in making an organization study, one should FIRST 33.____

A. review all the authoritative material in the field of government administration and organization
B. arrange the functions of the organization on a functional chart in accordance with the official documents
C. study the laws and authorities under which the organization operates
D. outline the purposes for which the organization study was originally established

34. His attitude is as provincial as an isolationist country's unwillingness to engage in any international trade whatever, on the ground that it will be required to buy something from outsiders which could possibly be produced by local talent, although not as well and not as cheaply. This statement is MOST descriptive of the attitude of the division chief in a government agency who 34.____

A. wishes to restrict promotions to supervisory positions in his division exclusively to employees in his division
B. refuses to delegate responsible tasks to subordinates qualified to perform these tasks
C. believes that informal on-the-job training of new staff members is superior to formal training methods
D. frequently makes personal issues out of matters that should be handled on an impersonal basis

35. A trainee was paid a weekly wage of $480.00 for a 40-hour work week. As a result of a new labor contract, he is paid $494.00 a week for a 38-hour work week with time-and-one-half pay for time worked in excess of 38 hours in any work week. 35.____
If he continues to work 40 hours weekly under the new contract, the amount by which his average hourly rate for a 40-hour work week under the new contract exceeds the hourly rate previously paid him lies between ______ and ______, inclusive.

A. $1.02; $1.06 B. $1.08; $1.16 C. $1.18; $1.26 D. $1.28; $1.36

36. The problem of inadequate storage space arising from the large number of inactive records stored in city agencies can be solved MOST satisfactorily with the aid of ______ equipment. 36.____

A. photostat
B. microfilm
C. IBM sorting
D. digital printing

37. To say that an employee is *erudite* means MOST NEARLY that he is 37.____

A. scholarly
B. insecure
C. efficient
D. punctual

38. The forms design section of a city agency recommended that the sizes of forms used by the agency be limited to the sizes that can be cut with the least amount of waste from either 17" x 22" or 17" x 28" sheets. 38.____
Of the following, the size that does NOT comply with this recommendation is

A. 4 1/2" x 5 1/2"
B. 3 3/4" x 4 1/4"
C. 3 1/2" x 4 1/4"
D. 4 1/4" x 2 3/4"

39. The number of investigations conducted by an agency in 2007 was 3,600. In 2008, the number of investigations conducted was one-third more than in 2007. The number of investigations conducted in 2009 was three-fourths of the number conducted in 2008. It is anticipated that the number of investigations conducted in 2010 will be equal to the average of the three preceding years. 39.____
On the basis of this information, the MOST accurate of the following statements is that the number of investigations conducted in

A. 2007 is larger than the number anticipated for 2010
B. 2008 is smaller than the number anticipated for 2010
C. 2009 is equal to the number conducted in 2007
D. 2009 is larger than the number anticipated for 2010

40. *The office manager thought it advisable to MOLLIFY his subordinate.* The word *mollify* as used in this sentence means MOST NEARLY 40.____

A. reprimand B. caution C. calm D. question

41. *The bureau chief adopted a DILATORY policy.* The word *dilatory* as used in this sentence means MOST NEARLY 41.____

A. tending to cause delay
B. acceptable to all affected
C. severe but fair
D. prepared with great care

42. *He complained about the PAUCITY of requests.* The word *paucity* as used in this sentence means MOST NEARLY 42.____

A. great variety
B. unreasonableness
C. unexpected increase
D. scarcity

43. To say that an event is *imminent* means MOST NEARLY that it is 43.____

A. near at hand
B. unpredictable
C. favorable or happy
D. very significant

44. *The general manager delivered a LAUDATORY speech.* The word *laudatory* as used in this sentence means MOST NEARLY 44.____

A. clear and emphatic
B. lengthy
C. introductory
D. expressing praise

45. *We all knew of his AVERSION for performing statistical work.* The word *aversion* as used in this sentence means MOST NEARLY 45.____

A. training
B. dislike
C. incentive
D. lack of preparation

46. *The engineer was CIRCUMSPECT in making his recommendations.* The word *circumspect* as used in this sentence means MOST NEARLY 46.____

A. hostile B. outspoken C. biased D. cautious

47. To say that certain clerical operations were *obviated* means MOST NEARLY that these operations were 47.____

A. extremely distasteful
B. easily understood
C. made unnecessary
D. very complicated

48. *The interviewer was impressed with the client's DEMEANOR.* The word *demeanor* as used in this sentence means MOST NEARLY 48.____

A. outward manner
B. plan of action
C. fluent speech
D. extensive knowledge

49. To say that the information was *gratuitous* means MOST NEARLY that it was 49.____

A. given freely
B. deeply appreciated
C. brief
D. valuable

50. *The supervisor was unaware of this EXIGENCY.* The word *exigency* as used in this sentence means MOST NEARLY 50.____

A. unexplained absence
B. costly delay
C. pressing need
D. final action

51. *She considered the supervisor's action to be ARBITRARY.* The word *arbitrary* as used in this sentence means MOST NEARLY 51.____

A. inconsistent
B. justifiable
C. appeasing
D. dictatorial

52. *His report on the activities of the agency was VERBOSE.* 52.____
The word *verbose* as used in this sentence means MOST NEARLY

A. vivid B. wordy C. vague D. oral

Questions 53-61.

DIRECTIONS: Questions 53 through 61 are to be answered SOLELY on the basis of the following information.

Assume that the following rules for computing service ratings are to be used experimentally in determining the service ratings of seven permanent employees. (Note that these rules are hypothetical and are NOT to be confused with the existing method of computing service ratings for employees.) The personnel record of each of these seven employees is given in Table II. You are to determine the answer to each of the questions on the basis of the rules given below for computing service ratings and the data contained in the personnel records of these seven employees.

All computations should be made as of the close of the rating period ending March 31, 2007.

RULES FOR COMPUTING SERVICE RATINGS

Service Rating

The service rating of each permanent competitive class employee shall be computed by adding the following three scores: (1) a basic score, (2) the employee's seniority score, and (3) the employee's efficiency score.

Seniority Score

An employee's seniority score shall be computed by crediting him with 1/2% per year for each year of service starting with the date of the employee's entrance as a permanent employee into the competitive class, up to a maximum of 15 years (7 1/2%). A residual fractional period of eight months or more shall be considered as a full year and credited with 1/2%. A residual fraction of from four to, but not including, eight months shall be considered as a half-year and credited with 1/4%. A residual fraction of less than four months shall receive no credit in the seniority score. For example, a person who entered the competitive class as a permanent employee on August 1, 1999 would, as of March 31, 2002, be credited with a seniority score of 1 1/2% for his two years and 8 months of service.

Efficiency Score

An employee's efficiency score shall be computed by adding the annual efficiency ratings received by him during his service in his PRESENT position. (Where there are negative efficiency ratings, such ratings shall be subtracted from the sum of the positive efficiency ratings.) An employee's annual efficiency rating shall be based on the grade he receives from his supervisor for his work performance during the annual efficiency rating period.

Basic Score

A basic score of 70% shall be given to each employee upon permanent appointment to a competitive class position.

An employee shall receive a grade of "A" for performing work of the highest quality and shall be credited with an efficiency rating of plus (+) 3%, An employee shall receive a grade of "F" for performing work of the lowest quality and shall receive an efficiency rating of minus (-) 2%. Table I, entitled "Basis for Determining Annual Efficiency Ratings," lists the six grades of work performance with their equivalent annual efficiency ratings. Table I also lists the efficiency ratings to be assigned for service in a position for less than a year during the annual efficiency rating period. The annual efficiency rating period shall run from April 1 to March 31, inclusive.

TABLE I

BASIS FOE DETERMINING ANNUAL EFFICIENCY RATINGS

		Annual Efficiency Rating for Service in a Position for:		
Quality of Work Performed	Grade Assigned A	8 months to a full year	At least 4 months but less than 8 months	Less than 4 months
Highest Quality	A	+ 3%	+1½%	0%
Good Quality	B	+ 2%	+ 1%	0%
Standard Quality	C	+ 1%	+½%	0%
Substandard Quality	D	0%	0%	0%
Poor Quality	E	-1%	-½%	0%
Lowest Quality	F	-2%	-1%	0%

Appointment or Promotion during an Efficiency Rating Period

An employee who has been appointed or promoted during an efficiency rating period shall receive for that period an efficiency rating only for work performed by him during the portion of the period that he served in the position to which he was appointed or promoted. His efficiency rating for the period shall be determined in accordance with Table I.

Sample Computation of Service Rating

John Smith entered the competitive class as a permanent employee on December 1, 2002 and was promoted to his present position as a Clerk, Grade 3 on November 1, 2005. As a Clerk, Grade 3, he received a grade of "B" for work performed during the five-month period extending from November 1, 2005 to March 31, 2006 and a grade of "C" for work performed during the full annual period extending from April 1, 2006 to March 32, 2007.

On the basis of the Rules for Computing Service Ratings, John Smith should be credited with:

70 % basic score
2 1/4% seniority score - for 4 years and 4 months of service (from 12-1-02 to 3-31-07)
2 % efficiency score - for 5 months of "B" service and a full year of "C" service
74 1/4%

TABLE II
PERSONNEL RECORD OF SEVEN PERMANENT COMPETITIVE CLASS EMPLOYEES

Employee	*Present Position*	*Date of Appointment or Promotion to Present Position*	*Date of Entry as Permanent Employee in Competitive Class*
Allen	*Clerk, Gr. 5*	*6-1-03*	*7-1-90*
Brown	*Clerk, Gr. 4*	*1-1-05*	*7-1-97*
Cole	*Clerk, Gr. 3*	*9-1-03*	*11-1-00*
Fox	*Clerk, Gr. 3*	*10-1-03*	*9-1-98*
Green	*Clerk, Gr. 2*	*12-1-01*	*12-1-01*
Hunt	*Clerk, Gr. 2*	*7-1-02*	*7-1-02*
Kane	*Steno, Gr. 3*	*11-16-04*	*3-1-01*

	Grades Received Annually for Work Performed in Present Position					
Employee	*4-1-01 to 3-31-02*	*4-1-02 to 3-31-03*	*4-1-03 to 3-31-04*	*4-1-04 to 3-31-05*	*4-1-05 to 3-31-06*	*4-1- -06 to 3-31 -07*
Allen			*C **	*C*	*B*	*C*
Brown				*C**	*C*	*B*
Cole			*A**	*B*	*C*	*C*
Fox			*C**	*C*	*D*	*C*
Green	*C**	*D*	*C*	*D*	*C*	*C*
Hunt		*C**	*C*	*E*	*C*	*C*
Kane				*B**	*B*	*C*

Explanatory Notes:

** Served in present position for less than a full year during this rating period. (Note date of appointment, or promotion, to present period.)*

All seven employees have served continuously as permanent employees since their entry into the competitive class.

Questions 53 through 61 refer to the employees listed in Table II. You are to answer these questions SOLELY on the basis of the preceding Rules for Computing Service Ratings and on the information concerning these seven employees given in Table II. You are reminded that all computations are to be made as of the close of the rating period ending March 31, 2007. Candidates may find it helpful to arrange their computations on their scratch paper in an orderly manner since the computations for one question may also be utilized in answering another question.

53. The seniority score of Allen is 53.___

A. 74% B. 8 1/2% C. 8% D. 8 1/4%

54. The seniority score of Fox exceeds that of Cole by 54.___

A. 1 1/2% B. 2% C. 1% D. 3/4 1/4

55. The seniority score of Brown is 55.___

A. equal to Hunt's
B. twice Hunt's
C. more than Hunt's by 1 1/2%
D. less than Hunt's by 1/2%

56. Green's efficiency score is 56.___

A. twice that of Kane
B. equal to that of Kane
C. less than Kane's by 1/2%
D. less than Kane's by 1%

57. Of the following employees, the one who has the LOWEST efficiency score is 57.___

A. Brown B. Fox C. Hunt D. Kane

58. A comparison of Hunt's efficiency score with his seniority score reveals that his efficiency score is 58.___

A. less than his seniority score by 1/2%
B. less than his seniority score by 3/4%
C. equal to his seniority score
D. greater than his seniority score by 1/2%

59. Fox's service rating is 59.___

A. 72 1/2% B. 74% C. 76 1/2% D. 76 3/4%

60. Brown's service rating is 60.___

A. less than 78%
B. 78%
C. 78 1/4%
D. more than 78 1/4%

61. Cole's service rating exceeds Kane's by 61.___

A. less than 2%
B. 2%
C. 2 1/4%
D. more than 2 1/4%

Questions 62-71.

DIRECTIONS: Each of the sentences numbered 62 to 71 may be classified under one of the following four options:
(A) faulty; contains an error in grammar only
(B) faulty; contains an error in spelling only
(C) faulty; contains an error in grammar and an error in spelling
(D) correct; contains no error in grammar or in spelling

Examine each sentence carefully to determine under which of the above four options it is best classified. Then, in the correspondingly numbered space at the right, write the letter preceding the option which is the BEST of the four listed above.

62. A recognized principle of good management is that an assignment should be given to whomever is best qualified to carry it out. 62.____

63. He considered it a privilege to be allowed to review and summarize the technical reports issued annually by your agency. 63.____

64. Because the warehouse was in an inaccessable location, deliveries of electric fixtures from the warehouse were made only in large lots. 64.____

65. Having requisitioned the office supplies, Miss Brown returned to her desk and resumed the computation of petty cash disbursements. 65.____

66. One of the advantages of this chemical solution is that records treated with it are not inflammable. 66.____

67. The complaint of this employee, in addition to the complaints of the other employees, were submitted to the grievance committee. 67.____

68. A study of the duties and responsibilities of each of the various categories of employees was conducted by an unprejudiced classification analyst. 68.____

69. Ties of friendship with this subordinate compels him to withold the censure that the subordinate deserves. 69.____

70. Neither of the agencies are affected by the decision to institute a program for rehabilitating physically handicaped men and women. 70.____

71. The chairman stated that the argument between you and he was creating an intolerable situation. 71.____

Questions 72-75.

DIRECTIONS: Each of Questions 72 through 75 consists of a statement containing five words in capital letters. One of these capitalized words is not in keeping with the meaning which the statement is evidently intended to convey. The five words in capital letters in each statement are reprinted after the statement. In the correspondingly numbered space at the right, write the letter preceding the one of the five words which does MOST to spoil the true meaning of the statement.

72. The alert employee will find, EVEN in the best managed offices, violations of some of the rules of good office management. However, further study will reveal that the correction of such violations is by ALL means a SIMPLE matter, BUT requires research, time, patience, and often a high degree of MANAGERIAL ability. 72.____

A. Even
B. All
C. Simple
D. But
E. Managerial

73. The information clerk in any organization must DELEGATE tact, courtesy, and good judgment in DEALING with callers, many of whom, on the other hand, DISREGARD business ETIQUETTE in their CONTACT with the information clerk. 73.____

A. Delegate
B. Dealing
C. Disregard
D. Etiquette
E. Contact

74. When the supervisor gives advancement or other rewards only to SUBORDINATES who have REQUESTED them, or shows a sincere INTEREST in the welfare of his staff, he is building FAVORABLE ATTITUDES. 74.____

A. Subordinates
B. Requested
C. Interest
D. Favorable
E. Attitudes

75. An appointee to the City's civil service must be a bona fide resident of the City for at least three years immediately prior to his APPOINTMENT. An appointee who served in the Armed Forces retains as his legal address that place where he resided prior to his ENTRY into the MILITARY service, PROVIDED he has taken definite action to establish a new RESIDENCE. 75.____

A. Appointment
B. Entry
C. Military
D. Provided
E. Residence

KEY (CORRECT ANSWERS)

1.	D	16.	D	31.	B	46.	D	61.	A
2.	B	17.	C	32.	D	47.	C	62.	A
3.	B	18.	B	33.	C	48.	A	63.	D
4.	A	19.	C	34.	A	49.	A	64.	B
5.	C	20.	D	35.	D	50.	C	65.	D
6.	A	21.	D	36.	B	51.	D	66.	B
7.	C	22.	C	37.	A	52.	B	67.	A
8.	B	23.	A	38.	B	53.	A	68.	D
9.	A	24.	B	39.	C	54.	C	69.	C
10.	D	25.	A	40.	C	55.	B	70.	C
11.	B	26.	B	41.	A	56.	C	71.	A
12.	C	27.	B	42.	D	57.	B	72.	B
13.	A	28.	D	43.	A	58.	D	73.	A
14.	B	29.	A	44.	D	59.	D	74.	B
15.	D	30.	C	45.	B	60.	B	75.	D

READING COMPREHENSION
UNDERSTANDING AND INTERPRETING WRITTEN MATERIAL

EXAMINATION SECTION

TEST 1

DIRECTIONS: Each question or incomplete statement is followed by several suggested answers or completions. Select the one that BEST answers the question or completes the statement. *PRINT THE LETTER OF THE CORRECT ANSWER IN THE SPACE AT THE RIGHT.*

Questions 1-4.

DIRECTIONS: Questions 1 through 4 are to be answered SOLELY on the basis of the following paragraph.

An annual leave allowance, which combines leaves previously given for vacation, personal business, family illness, and other reasons shall be granted members. Calculation of credits for such leave shall be on an annual basis beginning January 1st of each year. Annual leave credits shall be based on time served by members during preceding calendar year. However, when credits have been accrued and member retires during current year, additional annual leave credits shall, in this instance, be granted at accrual rate of three days for each completed month of service, excluding terminal leave. If accruals granted for completed months of service extend into following month, member shall be granted an additional three days accrual for completed month. This shall be the only condition where accruals in a current year are granted for vacation period in such year.

1. According to the above paragraph, if a fireman's wife were to become seriously ill so that he would take time off from work to be with her, such time off would be deducted from his _____ leave allowance. 1.____
   A. annual
   B. vacation
   C. personal business
   D. family illness

2. Terminal leave means leave taken 2.____
   A. at the end of the calendar year
   B. at the end of the vacation year
   C. immediately before retirement
   D. before actually earned, because of an emergency

3. A fireman appointed on July 1, 2017 will be able to take his first full or normal annual leave during the period 3.____
   A. July 1, 2017 to June 30, 2018
   B. Jan. 1, 2018 to Dec. 31, 2018
   C. July 1, 2018 to June 30, 2019
   D. Jan. 1, 2019 to Dec. 31, 2019

4. According to the above paragraph, a member who retires on July 15 of this year will be entitled to receive leave allowance based on this year of _____ days. 4.____
   A. 15
   B. 18
   C. 22
   D. 24

5. Fire alarm boxes are electromechanical devices for transmitting a coded signal. In each box, there is a trainwork of wheels. When the box is operated, a spring-activated code wheel begins to revolve. The code number of the box is etched on the circumference of the code wheel, and the latter is associated with the circuit in such a way that when it revolves it causes the circuit to open and close in a predetermined manner, thereby transmitting its particular signal to the central station. A fire alarm box is nothing more than a device for interrupting the flow of current in a circuit in such a way as to produce a coded signal that may be decoded by the dispatchers in the central office. 5.____
Based on the above, select the FALSE statement.
   A. Each standard fire alarm box has its own code wheel.
   B. The code wheel operates when the box is pulled.
   C. The code wheel is operated electrically.
   D. Only the break in the circuit by the notched wheel causes the alarm signal to be transmitted to the central office.

Questions 6-9.

DIRECTIONS: Questions 6 through 9 are to be answered SOLELY on the basis of the following paragraph.

Ventilation, as used in firefighting operations, means opening up a building or structure in which a fire is burning to release the accumulated heat, smoke, and gases. Lack of knowledge of the principles of ventilation on the part of firemen may result in unnecessary punishment due to ventilation being neglected or improperly handled. While ventilation itself extinguishes no fires, when used in an intelligent manner, it allows firemen to get at the fire more quickly, easily, and with less danger and hardship.

6. According to the above paragraph, the MOST important result of failure to apply the principles of ventilation at a fire may be 6.____
   A. loss of public confidence
   B. waste of water
   C. excessive use of equipment
   D. injury to firemen

7. It may be inferred from the above paragraph that the CHIEF advantage of ventilation is that it 7.____
   A. eliminates the need for gas masks
   B. reduces smoke damage
   C. permits firemen to work closer to the fire
   D. cools the fire

8. Knowledge of the principles of ventilation, as defined in the above paragraph, would be LEAST important in a fire in a 8.____
   A. tenement house
   B. grocery store
   C. ship's hold
   D. lumberyard

9. We may conclude from the above paragraph that for the well-trained and equipped fireman, ventilation is 9.____
   A. a simple matter
   B. rarely necessary
   C. relatively unimportant
   D. a basic tool

Questions 10-13.

DIRECTIONS: Questions 10 through 13 are to be answered SOLELY on the basis of the following passage.

Fire exit drills should be established and held periodically to effectively train personnel to leave their working area promptly upon proper signal and to evacuate the building, speedily but without confusion. All fire exit drills should be carefully planned and carried out in a serious manner under rigid discipline so as to provide positive protection in the event of a real emergency. As a general rule, the local fire department should be furnished advance information regarding the exact date and time the exit drill is scheduled. When it is impossible to hold regular drills, written instructions should be distributed to all employees.

Depending upon individual circumstances, fires in warehouses vary from those of fast development that are almost instantly beyond any possibility of employee control to others of relatively slow development where a small readily attackable flame may be present for periods of time up to 15 minutes or more during which simple attack with fire extinguishers or small building hoses may prevent the fire development. In any case, it is characteristic of many warehouse fires that at a certain point in development they flash up to the top of the stack, increase heat quickly, and spread rapidly. There is a degree of inherent danger in attacking warehouse type fires, and all employees should be thoroughly trained in the use of the types of extinguishers or small hoses in the buildings and well instructed in the necessity of always staying between the fire and a direct pass to an exit.

10. Employees should be instructed that, when fighting a fire, they MUST 10.____
    A. try to control the blaze
    B. extinguish any fire in 15 minutes
    C. remain between the fire and a direct passage to the exit
    D. keep the fire between themselves and the fire exit

11. Whenever conditions are such that regular fire drills cannot be held, then which one of the following actions should be taken? 11.____
    A. The local fire department should be notified.
    B. Rigid discipline should be maintained during work hours.
    C. Personnel should be instructed to leave their working area by whatever means are available.
    D. Employees should receive fire drill procedures in writing.

12. The above passage indicates that the purpose of fire exit drills is to train employees to 12.____
    A. control a fire before it becomes uncontrollable
    B. act as firefighters
    C. leave the working area promptly
    D. be serious

13. According to the above passage, fire exit drills will prove to be of UTMOST effectiveness if 13.____
    A. employee participation is made voluntary
    B. they take place periodically
    C. the fire department actively participates
    D. they are held without advance planning

Questions 14-16.

DIRECTIONS: Questions 14 through 16 are to be answered SOLELY on the basis of the following paragraph.

The heat output from unit heaters will depend on how fast and how completely dry hot steam fills the unit core. For complete and fast air removal and rapid drainage of condensate, use a trap actuated by water or vapor (inverted bucket trap) and not a trap operated by temperature only (thermostatic or bellows trap). A temperature-actuated trap will hold back the hot condensate until it cools to a point where the thermal element opens. When this happens, the condensate backs up in the heater and reduces the heat output. With a water-actuated trap, this will not happen as the water or condensate is discharged as fast as it is formed.

14. On the basis of the information given in the above paragraph, it can be concluded that the PROPER type of trap to use for a unit heater is a(n) _____ trap. 14.____
    A. thermostatic
    B bellows-type
    C. inverted bucket
    D. temperature

15. According to the above paragraph, the MAIN reason for using the type of trap specified for a unit heater is to 15.____
    A. bring the condensate up to steam temperature
    B. prevent reduction in the heat output of the unit heater
    C. permit cycling of the heater
    D. maintain constant temperature of condensate in the trap

16. As used in the above paragraph, the word *actuated* means MOST NEARLY 16.____
    A. clogged B. operated C. cleaned D. vented

Questions 17-25.

DIRECTIONS: Questions 17 through 25 are to be answered SOLELY on the basis of the following passage. Each question consists of a statement. You are to indicate whether the statement is TRUE (T) or FALSE (F).

MOVING AN OFFICE

An office with all its equipment is sometimes moved during working hours. This is a difficult task and must be done in an orderly manner to avoid confusion. The operation should be planned in such a way as not to interrupt the progress of work usually done in the office and to make possible the accurate placement of the furniture and records in the new location. If the office moves to a place inside the same building, the desks and files are moved with all their contents. If the movement is to another building, the contents of each desk and file are placed in boxes. Each box is marked with a letter showing the particular section in the new quarters to which it is to be moved. Also marked on each box is the number of the desk or file on which the box is to be placed. Each piece of equipment must have a numbered tag. The number of each piece of equipment is put in soft chalk on the floor in the new office to show the proper location, and several floor plans are made to show where each piece of equipment goes. When the moving is done, someone is stationed at each of the several exits of the old office to see that each box or piece of equipment has its destination clearly marked on it. At the new office, someone stands at each of the several entrances with a copy of the floor plan and directs the placing of the furniture and equipment according to the floor plan. No one should interfere at this point with the arrangements shown on the plan. Improvements in arrangement can be considered and made at a later date.

17. It is a hard job to move an office from one place to another during working hours. 17.____

18. Confusion cannot be avoided if an office is moved during working hours. 18.____

19. The work usually done in an office must be stopped for the day when the office is moved during working hours. 19.____

20. If an office is moved from one floor to another in the same building, the contents of a desk are taken out and put into boxes for moving. 20.____

21. If boxes are used to hold material from desks when moving an office, the box is numbered the same as the desk on which it is to be put. 21.____

22. Letters are marked in soft chalk on the floor at the new quarters to show where the desks should go when moved. 22.____

23. When the moving begins, a person is put at each exit of the old office to check that each box and piece of equipment has clearly marked on it where to go. 23.____

24. A person stationed at each entrance of the new quarters to direct the placing of the furniture and equipment has a copy of the floor plan of the new quarters. 24.____

25. If, while the furniture is being moved into the new office, a person helping at a doorway gets an idea of a better way to arrange the furniture, he should change the planned arrangement and make a record of the change. 25.____

KEY (CORRECT ANSWERS)

1.	A	11.	D
2.	C	12.	C
3.	D	13.	B
4.	B	14.	C
5.	C	15.	B
6.	D	16.	B
7.	C	17.	T
8.	D	18.	F
9.	D	19.	F
10.	C	20.	F

21.	T
22.	F
23.	T
24.	T
25.	F

TEST 2

DIRECTIONS: Each question or incomplete statement is followed by several suggested answers or completions. Select the one that BEST answers the question or completes the statement. *PRINT THE LETTER OF THE CORRECT ANSWER IN THE SPACE AT THE RIGHT.*

Questions 1-4.

DIRECTIONS: Questions 1 through 4 are to be answered SOLELY on the basis of the following paragraph.

In all cases of homicide, members of the Police Department who investigate will make every effort to obtain statements from dying persons. Such statements are of the greatest importance to the District Attorney. In many cases, there may be a failure to solve the crime if they are not taken. The principal element to be considered in taking the declaration of a dying person is his mental attitude. In order to be admissible in evidence, the person must have no hope of recovery. The patient will be fully interrogated on that point before a statement is taken.

1. In cases of homicide, according to the above paragraph, members of the police force will 1.____
   A. try to change the mental attitude of the dying person
   B. attempt to obtain a statement from the dying person
   C. not give the information they obtain directly to the District Attorney
   D. be careful not to injure the dying person unnecessarily

2. The mental attitude of the person making the dying statement is of GREAT importance because it can determine, according to the above paragraph, whether the 2.____
   A. victim should be interrogated in the presence of witnesses
   B. victim will be willing to make a statement of any kind
   C. statement will tell the District Attorney who committed the crime
   D. the statement can be used as evidence

3. District Attorneys find that statements of a dying person are important, according to the above paragraph, because 3.____
   A. it may be that the victim will recover and then refuse to testify
   B. they are important elements in determining the mental attitude of the victim
   C. they present a point of view
   D. it may be impossible to punish the criminal without such a statement

4. A well-known gangster is found dying from a bullet wound. The patrolman first on the scene, in the presence of witnesses, tells the man that he is going to die and asks, *Who shot you?* The gangster says, *Jones shot me, but he hasn't killed me. I'll live to get him.* He then falls back dead. According to the above paragraph, this statement is 4.____
   A. *admissible* in evidence; the man was obviously speaking the truth
   B. *not admissible* in evidence; the man obviously did not believe that he was dying

C. *admissible* in evidence; there were witnesses to the statement
D. *not admissible* in evidence; the victim did not sign any statement and the evidence is merely hearsay

Questions 5-7.

DIRECTIONS: Questions 5 through 7 are to be answered SOLELY on the basis of the following paragraph.

The factors contributing to crime and delinquency are varied and complex. The home and its immediate environment have been found to be crucial in determining the behavior patterns of the individual, and criminality can frequently be traced to faulty family relationships and a bad neighborhood. But in the search for a clearer understanding of the underlying causes of delinquent and criminal behavior, the total environment must be taken into consideration.

5. According to the above paragraph, family relationships 5.____
   A. tend to become faulty in bad neighborhoods
   B. are important in determining the actions of honest people as well as criminals
   C. are the only important element in the understanding of causes of delinquency
   D. are determined by the total environment

6. According to the above paragraph, the causes of crime and delinquency are 6.____
   A. not simple
   B. not meaningless
   C. meaningless
   D. simple

7. According to the above paragraph, faulty family relationships FREQUENTLY are 7.____
   A. responsible for varied and complex results
   B. caused when one or both parents have a criminal behavior pattern
   C. independent of the total environment
   D. the cause of criminal acts

Questions 8-10.

DIRECTIONS: Questions 8 through 10 are to be answered SOLELY on the basis of the following paragraph.

A change in the specific problems which confront the police and in the methods for dealing with them has taken place in the last few decades. The automobile is a two-way symbol of this change in policing. It menaces every city with a complicated traffic problem and has speeded up the process of committing a crime and making a getaway, but at the same time has increased the effectiveness of police operations. However, the major concern of police departments continues to be the antisocial or criminal actions and behavior of human beings.

8. On the basis of the above paragraph, it can be stated that, for the most part, in the past few decades the specific problems of a police force 8.____
   A. have changed but the general problems have not
   B. as well as the general problems have changed
   C. have remained the same but the general problems have changed
   D. as well as the general problems have remained the same

9. According to the above paragraph, advances in science and industry have, in general, made the police 9.____
   A. operations less effective from the overall point of view
   B. operations more effective from the overall point of view
   C. abandon older methods of solving police problems
   D. concern themselves more with the antisocial acts of human beings

10. The automobile is a *two-way symbol*, according to the above paragraph, because its use 10.____
    A. has speeded up getting to and away from the scene of a crime
    B. both helps and hurts police operations
    C. introduces a new antisocial act—traffic violation—and does away with criminals like horse thieves
    D. both increases and decreases speed by introducing traffic problems

Questions 11-14.

DIRECTIONS: Questions 11 through 14 are to be answered SOLELY on the basis of the following passage on INSTRUCTIONS TO COIN AND TOKEN CASHIERS.

INSTRUCTIONS TO COIN AND TOKEN CASHIERS

Cashiers should reset the machine registers to an even starting number before commencing the day's work. Money bags received directly from collecting agents shall be counted and receipted for on the collecting agent's form. Each cashier shall be responsible for all coin or token bags accepted by him. He must examine all bags to be used for bank deposits for cuts and holes before placing them in use. Care must be exercised so that bags are not cut in opening them. Each bag must be opened separately and verified before another bag is opened. The machine register must be cleared before starting the count of another bag. The amount shown on the machine register must be compared with the amount on the bag tag. The empty bag must be kept on the table for re-examination should there be a difference between the amount on the bag tag and the amount on the machine register.

11. A cashier should BEGIN his day's assignment by 11.____
    A. counting and accepting all money bags
    B. resetting the counting machine register
    C. examining all bags for cuts and holes
    D. verifying the contents of all money bags

12. In verifying the amount of money in the bags received from the collecting agent, it is BEST to 12.____
    A. check the amount in one bag at a time
    B. base the total on the amount on the collecting agent's form
    C. repeat the total shown on the bag tag
    D. refer to the bank deposit receipt

13. A cashier is instructed to keep each empty coin bag on his table while verifying its contents CHIEFLY because, as long as the bag is on the table 13.____
    A. it cannot be misplaced
    B. the supervisor can see how quickly the cashier works
    C. cuts and holes are easily noticed
    D. a recheck is possible in case the machine count disagrees with the bag tag total

14. The INSTRUCTIONS indicate that it is NOT proper procedure for a cashier to 14.____
    A. assume that coin bags are free of cuts and holes
    B. compare the machine register total with the total shown on the bag tag
    C. sign a form when he receives coin bags
    D. reset the machine register before starting the day's counting

Questions 15-17.

DIRECTIONS: Questions 15 through 17 are to be answered SOLELY on the basis of the following passage.

The mass media are an integral part of the daily life of virtually every American. Among these media the youngest, television, is the most pervasive. Ninety-five percent of American homes have at least one T.V. set, and on the average that set is in use for about 40 hours each week. The central place of television in American life makes this medium the focal point of a growing national concern over the effects of media portrayals of violence on the values, attitudes, and behavior of an ever-increasing audience.

In our concern about violence and its causes, it is easy to make television a scapegoat. But we emphasize the fact that there is no simple answer to the problem of violence—no single explanation of its causes, and no single prescription for its control. It should be remembered that America also experienced high levels of crime and violence in periods before the advent of television.

The problem of balance, taste and artistic merit in entertaining programs on television are complex. We cannot countenance government censorship of television. Nor would we seek to impose arbitrary limitations on programming which might jeopardize television's ability to deal in dramatic presentations with controversial social issues. Nonetheless, we are deeply troubled by television's constant portrayal of violence, not in any genuine attempt to focus artistic expression on the human condition, but rather in pandering to a public preoccupation with violence that television itself has helped to generate,

15. According to the above passage, television uses violence MAINLY 15.____
    A. to highlight the reality of everyday existence
    B. to satisfy the audience's hunger for destructive action

C. to shape the values and attitudes of the public
D. when it films documentaries concerning human conflict

16. Which one of the following statements is BEST supported by the above passage? 16.____
A. Early American history reveals a crime pattern which is not related to television.
B. Programs should give presentations of social issues and never portray violent acts.
C. Television has proven that entertainment programs can easily make the balance between taste and artistic merit a simple matter.
D. Values and behavior should be regulated by governmental censorship.

17. Of the following, which word has the same meaning as *countenance*, as used in the above passage? 17.____
A. Approve B. Exhibit C. Oppose D. Reject

Questions 18-21.

DIRECTIONS: Questions 18 through 21 are to be answered SOLELY on the basis of the following passage.

Maintenance of leased or licensed areas on public parks or land has always been a problem. A good rule to follow in the administration and maintenance of such areas is to limit the responsibility of any lessee or licensee to the maintenance of the structures and grounds essential to the efficient operation of the concession, not including areas for the general use of the public, such as picnic areas, public comfort stations, etc.; except where such facilities are leased to another public agency or where special conditions make such inclusion practicable, and where a good standard of maintenance can be assured and enforced. If local conditions and requirements are such that public use areas are included, adequate safeguards to the public should be written into contracts and enforced in their administration, to insure that maintenance by the concessionaire shall be equal to the maintenance standards for other park property.

18. According to the above passage, when an area on a public park is leased to a concessionaire, it is usually BEST to 18.____
A. confine the responsibility of the concessionaire to operation of the facilities and leave the maintenance function to the park agency
B. exclude areas of general public use from the maintenance obligation of the concessionaire
C. make the concessionaire responsible for maintenance of the entire area including areas of general public use
D. provide additional comfort station facilities for the area

19. According to the above passage, a valid reason for giving a concessionaire responsibility for maintenance of a picnic area within his leased area is that 19.____
A. local conditions and requirements make it practicable
B. more than half of the picnic area falls within his leased area
C. the concessionaire has leased picnic facilities to another public agency
D. the picnic area falls entirely within his leased area

20. According to the above passage, a precaution that should be taken when a concessionaire is made responsible for maintenance of an area of general public use in a park is 20.____
    A. making sure that another public agency has not previously been made responsible for this area
    B. providing the concessionaire with up-to-date equipment, if practicable
    C. requiring that the concessionaire take out adequate insurance for the protection of the public
    D. writing safeguards to the public into the contract

KEY (CORRECT ANSWERS)

1.	B	11.	B
2.	D	12.	A
3.	D	13.	D
4.	B	14.	A
5.	B	15.	B
6.	A	16.	A
7.	D	17.	A
8.	A	18.	B
9.	B	19.	A
10.	B	20.	D

TEST 3

DIRECTIONS: Each question or incomplete statement is followed by several suggested answers or completions. Select the one that BEST answers the question or completes the statement. *PRINT THE LETTER OF THE CORRECT ANSWER IN THE SPACE AT THE RIGHT.*

Questions 1-5.

DIRECTIONS: Questions 1 through 5 are to be answered SOLELY on the basis of the following paragraph.

Physical inspections are an important tool for the examiner because he will have to decide the case in many instances on the basis of the inspection report. Most proceedings in a rent office are commenced by the filing of a written application or complaint by an interested party; that is, either the landlord or the tenant. Such an application or complaint must be filed in duplicate in order that the opposing party may be served with a copy of the application or complaint and thus be given an opportunity to answer and oppose it. Sometimes, a further opportunity is given the applicant to file a written rebuttal or reply to his adversary's answer. Often an examiner can make a determination or decision based on the written application, the answer, and the reply to the answer; and, of course, it would speed up operations if it were always possible to make decisions based on written documents only. Unfortunately, decisions can't always be made that way. There are numerous occasions where <u>disputed</u> issues of fact remain which cannot be <u>resolved</u> on the basis of the written statements of the parties. Typical examples are the following: The tenant claims that the refrigerator or stove or bathroom fixture is not functioning properly and the landlord denies this It is obvious that in such cases an inspection of the accommodations is almost the only means of resolving such disputed issues,

1. According to the above paragraph, 1.____
   A. physical inspections are made in all cases
   B. physical inspections are seldom made
   C. it is sometimes possible to determine the facts in a case without a physical inspection
   D. physical inspections are made when it is necessary to verify the examiner's determination

2. According to the above paragraph, in MOST cases, proceedings are started by a(n) 2.____
   A. inspector discovering a violation
   B. oral complaint by a tenant or landlord
   C. request from another agency, such as the Building Department
   D. written complaint by a tenant or landlord

3. According to the above paragraph, when a tenant files an application with the rent office, the landlord is 3.____
   A. not told about the proceeding until after the examiner makes his determination
   B. given the duplicate copy of the application

C. notified by means of an inspector visiting the premises
D. not told about the proceeding until after the inspector has visited the premises

4. As used in the above paragraph, the word *disputed* means MOST NEARLY 4.____
A. unsettled B. contested C. definite D. difficult

5. As used in the above paragraph, the word *resolved* means MOST NEARLY 5.____
A. settled B. fixed C. helped D. amended

Questions 6-10.

DIRECTIONS: Questions 6 through 10 are to be answered SOLELY on the basis of the following paragraph.

The examiner should order or request an inspection of the housing accommodations. His request for a physical inspection should be in writing, identify the accommodations and the landlord and the tenant, and specify precisely just what the inspector is to look for and report on. Unless this request is specific and lists in detail every item which the examiner wishes to be reported, the examiner will find that the inspection has not served its purpose and that even with the inspector's report, he is still in no position to decide the case due to loose ends which have not been completely tied up. The items that the examiner is interested in should be separately numbered on the inspection request and the same number referred to in the inspector's report. You can see what it would mean if an inspector came back with a report that did not cover everything. It may mean a tremendous waste of time and often require a re-inspection.

6. According to the above paragraph, the inspector makes an inspection on the order of 6.____
A. the landlord B. the tenant
C. the examiner D. both the landlord and the tenant

7. According to the above paragraph, the reason for numbering each item that an inspector reports on is so that 7.____
A. the report is neat
B. the report can be easily read and referred to
C. none of the examiner's requests for information is missed
D. the report will be specific

8. The one of the following items that is NOT necessarily included in the request for inspection is 8.____
A. location of dwelling B. name of landlord
C. item to be checked D. type of building

9. As used in the above paragraph, the word *precisely* means MOST NEARLY 9.____
A. exactly B. generally C. usually D. strongly

10. As used in the above paragraph, the words *in detail* mean MOST NEARLY 10.____
A. clearly B. item by item C. substantially D. completely

Questions 11-13.

DIRECTIONS: Questions 11 through 13 are to be answered SOLELY on the basis of the following passage.

The agreement under which a tenant rents property from a landlord is known as a lease. Generally speaking, leases are classified as either short-term or long-term in duration. They are further subdivided according to the method used to determine the amount of periodic rent payments. Of the following types of lease in use, the more commonly used ones are the following:

1. The straight or fixed lease is one in which rent may be paid in equal amounts throughout the duration of the lease. These are usually restricted to short-term leasing, or somewhat longer-term if clauses in the lease provide for periodic escalation of payments as the economy shifts.
2. Percentage leasing, used for short-term commercial leasing, provides the landlord with a stipulated percentage of a tenant's gross sales from goods and services sold on the premises, in addition to a fixed amount of rent.
3. The net lease, generally long-term (ten years or more), requires the tenant to pay all operating costs, including real estate taxes and insurance. In a net-net lease, the tenant further agrees to meet mortgage interest and principal payments.
4. An escalated lease, which is a long-term lease, requires rent to be of a stipulated base amount which periodically is subject to escalation in accordance with cost-of-living index scales, or in direct proportion to taxes, insurance, and operating costs.

11. Based on the information given in the passage, which type of lease is MOST likely to be advantageous to a landlord if there is a high rate of inflation? 11.____
______ lease.
A. Fixed B. Percentage C. Net D. Escalated

12. On the basis of thee above passage, which types of lease would generally be MOST suitable for a well-established textile company which requires permanent facilities for its large operations? 12.____
_____ lease and _____ lease.
A. Percentage; escalated
B. Escalated; net
C. Straight; net
D. Straight; percentage

13. According to the above passage, the ONLY type of lease which assures the same amount of rent throughout a specified interval is the _____ lease. 13.____
A. straight B. percentage C. net-net D. escalated

Questions 14-15.

DIRECTIONS: Questions 14 and 15 are to be answered SOLELY on the basis of the following passage.

If you like people, if you seek contact with them rather than hide yourself in a corner, if you study your fellow men sympathetically, if you try consistently to contribute something to their success and happiness, if you are reasonably generous with your thought and your time, if you have a partial reserve with everyone but a seeming reserve with no one, you will get along with your superiors, your subordinates, and the human race.

By the scores of thousands, precepts and platitudes have been written for the guidance of personal conduct. The odd part of it is that, despite all of this labor, most of the frictions in modern society arise from the individual's feeling of inferiority, his false pride, his vanity, his unwillingness to yield space to any other man and his consequent urge to throw his own weight around. Goethe said that the quality which best enables a man to renew his own life, in his relation to others, is his capability of renouncing particular things at the right moment in order warmly to embrace something new in the next.

14. On the basis of the above passage, it may be INFERRED that 14.____
   A. a person should be unwilling to renounce privileges
   B. a person should realize that loss of a desirable job assignment may come at an opportune moment
   C. it is advisable for a person to maintain a considerable amount of reserve in his relationship with unfamiliar people
   D. people should be ready to contribute generously to a worthy charity

15. Of the following, the MOST valid implication made by the above passage is that 15.____
   A. a wealthy person who spends a considerable amount of money entertaining his friends is not really getting along with them
   B. if a person studies his fellow men carefully and impartially, he will tend to have good relationships with them
   C. individuals who maintain seemingly little reserve in their relationships with people have in some measure overcome their own feelings of inferiority
   D. most precepts that have been written for the guidance of personal conduct in relationships with other people are invalid

Questions 16-17.

DIRECTIONS: Questions 16 and 17 are to be answered SOLELY on the basis of the following passage.

When a design for a new bank note of the Federal Government has been prepared by the Bureau of Engraving and Printing and has been approved by the Secretary of the Treasury, the engravers begin the work of cutting the design in steel. No one engraver does all the work. Each man is a specialist. One works only on portraits, another on lettering, another on scroll work, and so on. Each engraver, with a steel tool known as a graver, and aided by a powerful magnifying glass, carefully carves his portion of the design into the steel. He knows that one false cut or a slip of his tool, or one miscalculation of width or depth of line, may destroy the merit of his work. A single mistake means that months or weeks of labor will have been in vain. The bureau is proud of the fact that no counterfeiter ever has duplicated the excellent work of its expert engravers.

16. According to the above passage, each engraver in the Bureau of Engraving and Printing 16.____
   A. must be approved by the Secretary of the Treasury before he can begin work on the design for a new bank note
   B. is responsible for engraving a complete design of a new bank note by himself
   C. designs new bank notes and submits them for approval to the Secretary of the Treasury
   D. performs sonly a specific part of the work of engraving a design for a new bank note

17. According to the above passage, 17.____
   A. an engraver's tools are not available to a counterfeiter
   B. mistakes made in engraving a design can be corrected immediately with little delay in the work of the Bureau
   C. the skilled work of the engravers has not been successfully reproduced by counterfeiter
   D. careful carving and cutting by the engraver is essential to prevent damage to equipment

Questions 18-21.

DIRECTIONS: Questions 18 through 21 are to be answered SOLELY on the basis of the following passage.

In the late fifties, the average American housewife spent $4.50 per day for a family of four on food and 5.15 hours in food preparation, if all of her food was *home prepared*; she spent $5.80 per day and 3.245 hours if all of her food was purchased *partially prepared*; and $6.70 per day and 1.64 hours if all of her food was purchased *ready-to-serve*.

Americans spent about 20 billion dollars for food products in 1941. They spent nearly 70 billion dollars in 1958. They spent 25 percent of their cash income on food in 1958. For the same kinds and quantities of food that consumers bought in 1941, they would have spent only 16% of their cash income in 1958. It is obvious that our food does cost more. Many factors contribute to this increase besides the additional cost that might be attributed to processing. Consumption of more expensive food items, higher marketing margins, and more food eaten in restaurants are other factors.

The Census of Manufacturers gives some indication of the total bill for processing. The value added by manufacturing of food and kindred products amounted to 3.5 billion of the 20 billion dollars spent for food in 1941. In the year 1958, the comparable figure had climbed to 14 billion dollars.

18. According to the above passage, the cash income of Americans in 1958 was MOST NEARLY _____ billion dollars. 18.____
   A. 11.2 B. 17.5 C. 70 D. 280

19. According to the above passage, if Americans bought the same kinds and quantities of food in 1958 as they did in 1941, they would have spent MOST NEARLY _____ billion dollars. 19.____
   A. 20 B. 45 C. 74 D. 84

20. According to the above passage, the percent increase in money spent for food in 1958 over 1941, as compared with the percentage increase in money spent for food processing in the same years, 20.____
   A. was greater
   B. was less
   C. was the same
   D. cannot be determined from the passage

21. In 1958, an American housewife who bought all of her food ready-to-serve saved time, as compared with the housewife who prepared all of her food at home 21.____
   A. 1.6 hours daily
   B. 1.9 hours daily
   C. 3.5 hours daily
   D. an amount of time which cannot be determined from the above passage

Questions 22-25.

DIRECTIONS: Questions 22 through 25 are to be answered SOLELY on the basis of the following passage.

Any member of the retirement system who is in city service, who files a proper application for service credit and agrees to deductions from his compensation at triple his normal rate of contribution, shall be credited with a period of city service previous to the beginning of his present membership in the retirement system. The period of service credited shall be equal to the period throughout which such triple deductions are made, but may not exceed the total of the city service the number rendered between his first day of eligibility for membership in the retirement system and the day he last became a member. After triple contributions for all of the first three years of service credit claimed, the remaining service credit may be purchased by a single payment of the sum of the remaining payments. If the total time purchasable exceeds ten years, triple contributions may be made for one-half of such time, and the remaining time purchased by a single payment of the sum of the remaining payments. Credit for service acquired in the above manner may be used only in determining the amount of any retirement benefit. Eligibility for such benefit will, in all cases, be based upon service rendered after the employee's membership last began, and will be exclusive of service credit purchased as described above.

22. According to the above passage, in order to obtain credit for city service previous to the beginning of an employee's present membership in the retirement system, the employee must 22.____
   A. apply for the service credit and consent to additional contributions to the retirement system
   B. apply for the service credit before he renews his membership in the retirement system
   C. have previous city service which does not exceed ten years
   D. make contributions to the retirement system for three years

23. According to the information in the above passage, credit for city service previous to the beginning of an employee's present membership in the retirement system is 23.____
   A. credited up to a maximum of ten years
   B. credited to any member of the retirement system
   C. used in determining the amount of the employee's benefits
   D. used in establishing the employee's eligibility to receive benefits

24. According to the information in the above passage, a member of the retirement system may purchase service credit for 24.____
   A. the period of time between his first day of eligibility for membership in the retirement system and the date he applies for the service credit
   B. one-half of the total of his previous city service if the total time exceeds ten years
   C. the period of time throughout which triple deductions are made
   D. the period of city service between his first day of eligibility for membership in the retirement system and the day he last became a member

25. Suppose that a member of the retirement system has filed an application for service credit for five years of previous city service. 25.____
Based on the information in the above passage, the employee may purchase credit for this previous city service by making
   A. triple contributions for three years
   B. triple contributions for one-half of the time and a single payment of the sum of the remaining payments
   C. triple contributions for three years and a single payment of the sum of the remaining payments
   D. a single payment of the sum of the payments

KEY (CORRECT ANSWERS)

1. C
2. D
3. B
4. B
5. A

6. C
7. C
8. D
9. A
10. B

11. D
12. B
13. A
14. B
15. C

16. D
17. C
18. D
19. B
20. B

21. C
22. A
23. C
24. D
25. C

OFFICE RECORD KEEPING

EXAMINATION SECTION

TEST 1

DIRECTIONS: Each question or incomplete statement is followed by several suggested answers or completions. Select the one that BEST answers the question or completes the statement. *PRINT THE LETTER OF THE CORRECT ANSWER IN THE SPACE AT THE RIGHT.*

Questions 1-5.

DIRECTIONS: Questions 1 through 5 are to be answered on the basis of the following chart to check for address and zip code errors.

A. No errors
B. Address only
C. Zip code only
D. Both

	Correct List Address	Zip Code	List to be Checked Address	Zip Code	
1.	44-A Western Avenue Bethesda, MD	65564	44-A Western Avenue Bethesda, MD	65654	1.____
2.	567 Opera Lane Jackson, MO	28218	567 Opera Lane Jacksen, MO	28218	2.____
3.	200 W. Jannine Dr. Missoula, MT	30707	200 W. Jannine Dr. Missoula, MT	30307	3.____
4.	28 Champaline Dr. Reno, NV	34101	28 Champaine Way Reno, NV	43101	4.____
5.	65156 Rodojo Parsimony, KY	44590-7326	65156 Rodojo Parsimony, KY	44590-7326	5.____

6. When alphabetized correctly, which of the following would be second? 6.____
   A. flame B. herring C. decadence D. emoticon

7. Which one of the following letters is as far after E as K is before R in the alphabet? 7.____
   A. J B. K C. H D. M

8. How many pairs of the following sets of numbers are exactly alike? 8.____

134232	123456	432512	561343
564643	432123	132439	438318

   A. 0 B. 2 C. 3 D. 4

9. When alphabetized correctly, which of the following would be FOURTH? 9.____
   A. microcosm B. natural C. lithe D. nature

10. When alphabetized correctly, which of the following would be THIRD? 10.____
   A. exoskeleton B. euthanize C. Europe D. eurythmic

11. Which one of the following letters is as far before T as S is after I in the alphabet? 11.____
   A. j B. K C. M D. N

12. How many pairs of the following sets of letters are exactly ALIKE? 12.____

GIHEKE	GIHEKE
KIWNEB	KWINEB
PQMZJI	PMQZJI
OPZIBS	OBZIBS
PONEHE	POENHE

   A. 0 B. 1 C. 2 D. 4

13. When alphabetized correctly, which of the following would be FIRST? 13.____
   A. Catalina B. catcher C. caustic D. curious

14. Which of the following letters is as far after D as U is after B in the alphabet? 14.____
   A. R B. V C. W D. Z

Questions 15-19.

DIRECTIONS: Use the following information and chart to complete Questions 15 through 19.

Every theft reported to an adjuster needs to be assigned a six-letter code containing the following:

First Letter: Type of theft
Second Letter: Witnesses
Third Letter: Value of stolen item
Fourth Letter: Location
Fifth Letter: Time of theft
Sixth Letter: Elapsed between theft and report

<u>Type of Theft:</u>
A. Breaking and Entering
B. Retail Theft
C. Armed robbery
D. Grand Theft Auto

<u>Witnesses</u>
A. None
B. 1 witness
C. Multiple witnesses
D. Security camera

Location
A. Single Family Home
B. Apartment Building
C. Store
D. Office
E. Vehicle
F. Public Space (Parking Garage, Park, etc.)

Time Elapsed Between Theft and Report
A. 0-1 hour
B. 1-4 hours
C. 4-12 hours
D. 12-24 hours
E. 24 Hours

Time of Theft
A. 7 AM – 1 PM
B. 1 PM – 6 PM
C. 6 PM – 11 PM
D. 11 PM – 3 AM
E. 3 AM – 7 AM

Value of Stolen Items
A. $0-$100
B. $101-$250
C. $251-$500
D. $500-$1000
E. $1001-$5000
F. $5000 or more

15. At 9:30 PM, $175 worth of clothing was stolen from a store. The crime was reported right away by a single store associate. Which of the following would be the CORRECT code? 15.____
A. BCCABB B. BBBCCA C. ACCBAB D. CBCABB

16. A Crossover vehicle worth $4,500 was stolen from a park at approximately 6:45 AM this morning. It was reported stolen at 11:00 AM later that morning by the owner. There were no witnesses. What is the CORRECT code? 16.____
A. DEECAF B. CFECAE C. DEFECA D. DAEFEC

17. Although it was just reported, a breaking and entering occurred 5 days ago at 1:30 AM, according to security cameras that recorded the theft at the accounting firm. Although locks and doors were damaged, nothing was stolen. Which of the following would be the CORRECT code? 17.____
A. ADDEEA B. ADDDAE C. ADADDE D. ADEADE

18. Jill Wagner was held at knifepoint this morning at 11:30 AM when she was walking out of her apartment complex. The thief demanded money, and she gave him $54. She was the only witness and reported the crime immediately. Which of the following would be the CORRECT code? 18.____
A. CBABAA B. BBABAA C. CBBABB D. ABBBCA

19. An artifact worth $5,500 was stolen from the home of Chad Judea this early evening while he was out to dinner from 5:30 PM to 6 PM. When he arrived home at 6 PM, he immediately called the police. There were no witnesses. Which of the following would be the CORRECT code? 19.____
A. AABBAF B. AABFAF C. AABABF D. AAFABA

20. Diatribe means MOST NEARLY 20.____
A. argument B. cooperation C. delicate D. arrogance

21. Vitriolic means MOST NEARLY 21.____
    A. flammable B. fearful C. spiteful D. asinine

22. Aplomb means MOST NEARLY 22.____
    A. self-righteous B. respectable C. dispirited D. self-confidence

23. Pervicacious means MOST NEARLY 23.____
    A. rotten B. immoral C. stubborn D. immortal

24. Detrimental means MOST NEARLY 24.____
    A. valuable B. selfish C. hopeless D. harmful

25. Heinous means MOST NEARLY 25.____
    A. sweating B. glorious C. atrocious D. moderate

KEY (CORRECT ANSWERS)

1.	C	11.	A
2.	B	12.	B
3.	C	13.	A
4.	D	14.	C
5.	A	15.	B
6.	D	16.	D
7.	B	17.	C
8.	A	18.	A
9.	D	19.	D
10.	B	20.	A

21.	C
22.	D
23.	C
24.	D
25.	C

TEST 2

DIRECTIONS: Each question or incomplete statement is followed by several suggested answers or completions. Select the one that BEST answers the question or completes the statement. *PRINT THE LETTER OF THE CORRECT ANSWER IN THE SPACE AT THE RIGHT.*

Questions 1-7.

DIRECTIONS: In answering Questions 1 through 7, you will be presented with analogies (known as word relationships). Select the answer choice that BEST completes the analogy.

1. Coordinated is related to movement as speech is related to 1.____
   A. predictive B. rapid C. prophetic D. articulate

2. Pottery is related to shard as wood is related to 2.____
   A. acorn B. chair C. smoke D. kiln

3. Poverty is related to money as famine is related to 3.____
   A. nourishment B. infirmity C. illness D. care

4. Farmland is related to arable as waterway is related to 4.____
   A. impenetrable B. maneuverable
   C. fertile D. deep

5. 19 is related to 17 as 37 is related to 5.____
   A. 39 B. 36 C. 34 D. 31

6. Cup is related to lip as bird is related to 6.____
   A. beak B. grass C. forest D. bush

7. ZRYQ is related to KCJB as PWOV is related to 7.____
   A. GBHA B. ISJT C. ELDK D. EOFP

Questions 8-12.

DIRECTIONS: In answering Questions 8 through 12, each of the questions has a group. Find out which one of the given alternatives will be another member of that group.

8. Springfield, Sacramento, Tallahassee 8.____
   A. Buffalo B. Bangor C. Pittsburgh D. Providence

9. Lock, Shut, Fasten 9.____
   A. Window B. Iron C. Door D. Block

10. Pathology, Radiology, Ophthalmology 10.____
   A. Zoology B. Hematology C. Geology D. Biology

11. Karate, Jujitsu, Boxing 11.____
    A. Polo B. Pole-vault C. Judo D. Swimming

12. Newspaper, Hoarding, Television 12.____
    A. Press B. Rumor C. Media D. Broadcast

Questions 13-18.

DIRECTIONS: Questions 13 through 18 are to be answered on the basis of the following pie chart.

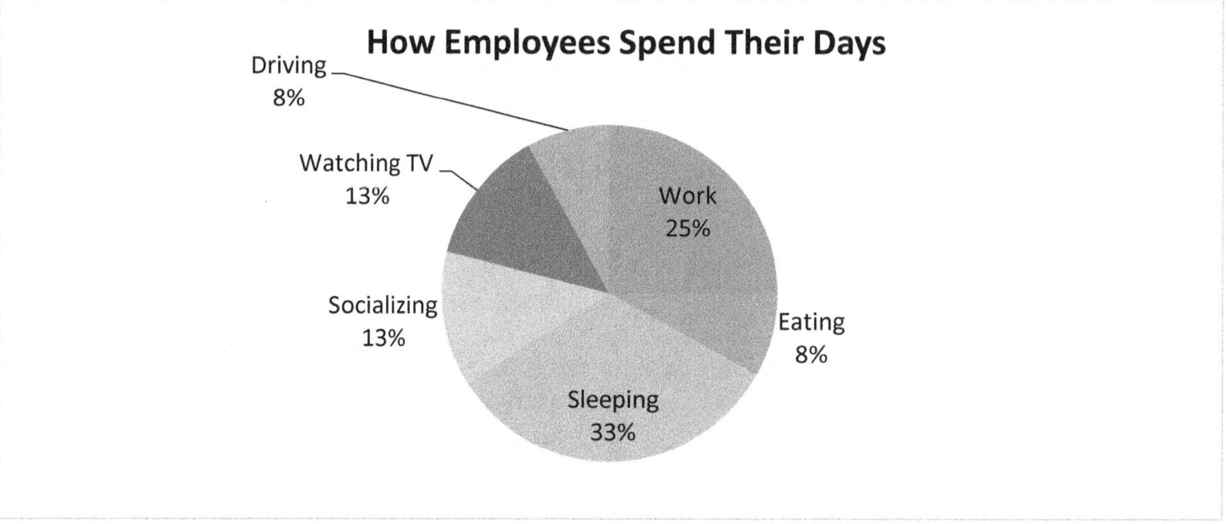

13. Approximately how many hours a day are spent eating? 13.____
    A. 2 hours B. 5 hours C. 1 hour D. 30 minutes

14. According to the graph, for each 48 hour period, about how many hours are spent socializing and watching TV? 14.____
    A. 9 hours B. 6 hours C. 12 hours D. 3 hours

15. If an employee ate two-thirds of their meals at a restaurant, what percentage of the total day is spent eating at home? 15.____
    A. 2.5% B. 5.3% C. 8% D. 1.4%

16. About how many hours a day are spent working and sleeping? 16.____
    A. 7 B. 10 C. 12 D. 14

17. Which of the following equations could be used to figure out how much time an employee spends watching TV during a week? T equals the total amount of time watching TV during the week. 17.____
    A. T = 13% x 24 x 7 B. T = 24 x 13 x 7
    C. T = 24/13% x 7 D. T = 1.3 x 7 x 24

18. How many hours a week does the average employee spend socializing? 18.____
    A. 20 B. 22 C. 23 D. 24

Questions 19-25.

DIRECTIONS: Questions 19 through 25 are to be answered on the basis of the following charts.

DIAL DIRECT	WEEKDAY FULL RATE		EVENING 40% DISCOUNT		WEEKEND 60% DISCOUNT	
SAMPLE RATES FROM SEATTLE TO	FIRST MINUTE	EACH ADDITIONAL MINUTE	FIRST MINUTE	EACH ADDITIONAL MINUTE	FIRST MINUTE	EACH ADDITIONAL MINUTE
Savannah, GA	.52	.23	.31	.14	.21	.08
Providence, RI	.52	.223	.31	.14	.21	.08
Golden, CO	.52	.23	.31	.14	.21	.08
Indianapolis, IN	.48	.19	.29	.11	.19	.07
San Diego, CA	.54	.24	.32	.14	.22	.09
Tallahassee, FL	.54	.24	.32	.14	.22	.09
Milwaukee, WI	.57	.27	.34	.16	.23	.09
Minneapolis, MN	.49	.22	.29	.13	.20	.08
Baton Rouge, LA	.52	.23	.31	.14	.21	.08
Buffalo, NY	.52	.23	.31	.14	.21	.08
Annapolis, MD	.54	.24	.32	.14	.22	.09
Washington, DC	.52	.23	.31	.14	.21	.08

OPERATOR ASSISTED		
STATION-TO-STATION		PERSON-TO-PERSON
1 – 10 MILES	$.75	$3.00 FEE FOR ALL MILEAGES
11 - 22 MILES	$1.10	*NOTE: Add to this base charge – the minute rates from the above chart
23-3000 MILES	$1.55	

19. What is the price of a 6-minute dial direct call to Annapolis, MD when you call on a weekend? 19.____
A. $0.59 B. $0.54 C. $0.67 D. $0.49

20. What is the difference in cost between a 10 minute dial direct to Buffalo, NY and a 10 minute person-to-person call to Buffalo, NY? 20.____
A. $1.55 B. $3.00 C. $0.55 D. $4.55

21. What is the price of a 15-minute operator-assisted Station-to-Station call to Indianapolis, IN on a Monday at noon? 21.____
A. $3.74 B. $7.80 C. $3.45 D. $4.69

22. What is the difference in price between an 11-minute dial direct call to Milwaukee, WI at 11:00 AM on a Wednesday and the same call made at 9 PM that night? 22.____
A. $2.27 B. $3.00 C. $1.55 D. $1.336

23. Which of the following is NOT a type of charge for a dial direct call? 23.____
    A. Holiday B. Evening C. Weekend D. Weekday

24. If a 3.5% tax applied to the total cost of any call, what would be the TOTAL cost of a 13-minute weekday, dial direct call to Golden, CO? 24.____
    A. $3.28 B. $3.39 C. $4.94 D. $6.39

25. What is the amount of discount from a dial direct, weekday call to Tallahassee, FL cost as compared to a dial direct, weekend call to Tallahassee? 25.____
    A. 45% B. 30% C. 60% D. 20%

KEY (CORRECT ANSWERS)

1.	D	11.	C
2.	B	12.	D
3.	A	13.	A
4.	C	14.	C
5.	D	15.	A
6.	A	16.	D
7.	C	17.	A
8.	D	18.	B
9.	D	19.	C
10.	B	20.	B

21.	D
22.	D
23.	A
24.	B
25.	C

TEST 3

DIRECTIONS: Each question or incomplete statement is followed by several suggested answers or completions. Select the one that BEST answers the question or completes the statement. *PRINT THE LETTER OF THE CORRECT ANSWER IN THE SPACE AT THE RIGHT.*

Questions 1-7.

DIRECTIONS: Questions 1 through 7 are to be answered on the basis of the following graph.

Corporate Fundraiser – Candy Sales by the Case

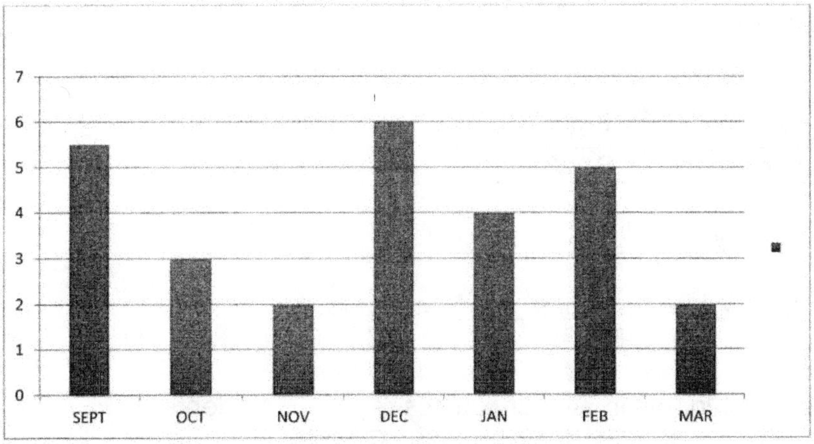

1. The vertical scale ranging from 0 to 7 represents the number of 1.____
   A. students selling candy
   B. candy sold in each case
   C. days each month that candy was sold
   D. cases of candy sold

2. Which two months had approximately the same amount of candy sold? 2.____
   A. November and March B. September and February
   C. November and October D. October and March

3. Which month showed a 100% increase in sales over the month of November? 3.____
   A. March B. January C. April D. December

4. From month-to-month, which month saw an approximate 33% drop in sales from the previous month? 4.____
   A. March B. September C. January D. October

5. The amount of candy sold in December is twice the amount of candy sold in which other month? 5.____
   A. October B. March C. January D. September

6. What was the total amount of candy sold during the months shown on the graph? 6.____
   A. 44 cases B. 35.5 cases C. 23.5 cases D. 27.5 cases

7. If the fundraiser extended the additional five months of the year and added an additional 65% in sales, approximately how many cases would be sold in total for an entire year? 7.____
   A. 40.5 cases B. 37 cases C. 45 cases D. 27.5 cases

Questions 8-11.

DIRECTIONS: Questions 8 through 11 are to be answered on the basis of the following chart.

S = 10 students
s = 5 students

Mr. Hucklebee	S S S S s
Ms. Shopenhauer	S S S
Mr. White	S S S s
Mrs. Mulrooney	S S S

8. The size of Mr. White's class is _____ students. 8.____
   A. 30 B. 35 C. 40 D. 4

9. The total of all students in all four classes is _____ students. 9.____
   A. 150 B. 140 C. 125 D. 14

10. The average class size based on the above chart is _____ students. 10.____
    A. 140 B. 45 C. 35 D. 30

11. In order to ensure each teacher has the same amount of students in each class, how many students would need to transfer out of Mr. Hucklebee's class? 11.____
    A. 10
    B. 5
    C. 0
    d. 15 would need to transfer into his class

12. When alphabetized correctly, which of the following would be THIRD? 12.____
    A. box B. departed C. electrical D. elemental

13. When alphabetized correctly, which of the following would be SECOND? 13.____
    A. polarize B. omnipotent C. polygraph D. omniscient

14. When alphabetized correctly, which of the following would be THIRD? 14.____
    A. Macklemore, Jonathan B. Mackelmore, J.
    C. DiCastro, Darian D. Castro, Darren Henry

15. The group fought through the fog, *shambling* through the night, doing their best to stay upright. 15.____
The word *shambling* means
A. frozen in place
B. running
C. walking awkwardly
D. shivering uncontrollably

16. Many doctors agree that Gen-aspirin is the best for fighting headaches. It comes in different flavors and is easy to swallow. 16.____
Is this a valid or invalid argument?
A. Invalid
B. Valid

Questions 17-21.

DIRECTIONS: Questions 17 through 21 are to be answered on the basis of the following paragraph.

Hospital workers and volunteers often ask Mr. Ansley to educate children who are hospitalized with primary ciliary dyskinesia (PCD). As he goes through the precautionary cleaning process (scrubbing, donning sterilized clothes, etc.) in order to see his students, Mr. Ansley wonders why their parents add the stress and pressure of schooling and trying to play catch-up because of the amount of time spent in the hospital and not in the classroom, which is an unfortunate side effect of patients with PCD. These children go through so many painful treatments on a given day that it seems punishing to subject them to schooling as normal children do, especially with life expectancy being as short as it is.

17. What is meant by *precautionary* in the second sentence? 17.____
A. Careful
B. Protective
C. Sterilizing
D. Medical

18. What is the MAIN idea of this passage? 18.____
A. The preparation to visit a patient with primary ciliary dyskinesia is extensive.
B. Children with PCD are unable to live normal lives.
C. Children with PCD die young.
D. Certain allowances should be made for children with PCD.

19. What is the author's purpose? 19.____
A. To advise
B. To educate
C. To establish credibility
D. To amuse

20. What is the author's tone? 20.____
A. Cruel
B. Sympathetic
C. Disbelieving
D. Cheerful

21. How is Mr. Ansley so familiar with the procedures used when visiting a child with PCD? 21.____
A. He has read about it
B. He works in the hospital.
C. His child has PCD.
D. He tutors them on a regular basis.

Questions 22-25.

DIRECTIONS: One of the underlined words in Questions 22 through 25 should be changed. Select the one that should be changed and print the letter of the word that would change the underlined word.

22. After we washed the fruit that had growing in the garden, we knew there was a store that would buy them. 22.____
A. washing B. grown C. is D. No change

23. When the temperature drops under 32 degrees (F), the water on the lake freezes, which allowed children to skate across it. 23.____
A. dropped B. froze C. allows D. No change

24. My friend's bulldog, while chasing cars in the street, always manages to knock over our garbage bins. 24.____
A. chased B. manage C. knocks D. No change

25. Some of the ice on the driveway has melted. 25.____
A. having melted
B. have melted
C. has melt
D. No change

KEY (CORRECT ANSWERS)

1.	D	11.	A
2.	A	12.	C
3.	B	13.	D
4.	C	14.	B
5.	A	15.	C
6.	D	16.	A
7.	C	17.	C
8.	B	18.	D
9.	B	19.	A
10.	C	20.	B

21.	D
22.	B
23.	C
24.	D
25.	D

TEST 4

DIRECTIONS: Each question or incomplete statement is followed by several suggested answers or completions. Select the one that BEST answers the question or completes the statement. *PRINT THE LETTER OF THE CORRECT ANSWER IN THE SPACE AT THE RIGHT.*

Questions 1-2.

DIRECTIONS: One of the underlined words in Questions 1 and 2 should be changed. Select the one that should be changed and print the letter of the word that would change the underlined word.

1. <u>You</u> can get to Martha's Vineyard by driving from Boston to Woods Hole. Once there, you can travel over on a boat, but <u>you</u> may find traveling by airplane to be more exciting. 1.____
   A. they B. visitors C. it D. No change

2. When John wants to go to the store looking for <u>milk and eggs</u>, <u>you</u> must remember to bring <u>his</u> wallet. 2.____
   A. them B. he C. its D. No change

3. An item that sells for \$400 is put on sale at \$145. What is the percentage of decrease? 3.____
   A. 25% B. 28% C. 64% D. 36%

4. Two Junior College Mathematics courses have a total of 510 students. The 9:00 AM class has 60 more than the 12:30 PM class. How many students are in the 12:30 class? 4.____
   A. 225 B. 285 C. 255 D. 205

5. If a car gets 26 miles per gallon and it has driven 75,210 miles, approximately what is the number of gallons of gas that it has used? 5.____
   A. 3,000 B. 2,585 C. 165 D. 1,800

6. Which one of the following sentences about proper telephone usage is NOT always correct? When answering a telephone, you should 6.____
   A. know who you are speaking to
   B. give the caller your undivided attention
   C. identify yourself to the caller
   D. obtain the information your caller wishes before you do other work

7. You are part of the "Safety at Work" committee, which is dedicated to ensuring safety of employees. During your regular shift, you notice an employee in violation of one of your committee's rules. Which of the following actions should you take FIRST? 7.____
   A. Speak with the employee about the safety rules and mandate them to stop breaking the rules.
   B. Speak to the employee about safety rules and point out the rule they violated.
   C. Bring up the issue during the next committee meeting.
   D. Report the violation to the employee's superiors.

8. Part of your duties is overseeing employee confidential information. A friend and coworker of yours asks to obtain information concerning another employee. Which is the BEST action to take? 8.____
   A. Ask the coworker if you can share the information.
   B. Ask your supervisor if you can give the information to your friend.
   C. Refuse to give the information to your friend.
   D. Give the information to your friend.

9. Which of the following words means the OPPOSITE of protract? 9.____
   A. Extend B. Hesitant C. Curtail D. Plethora

10. Which of the following words means the OPPOSITE of conserve? 10.____
    A. Relinquish B. Waste C. Proficient D. Rigid

11. Which of the following words means the SAME as dissipate? 11.____
    A. Scatter B. Emancipate
    C. Engage D. Accumulate

12. Your office just purchased 14 fax machines. Each fax machine costs $79.99. How much did the 14 fax machines cost? 12.____
    A. $1,119.86 B. $1,108.77 C. $1,201.44 D. $1,788.22

Questions 13-19.

DIRECTIONS: Questions 13 through 19 are to be answered on the basis of the following chart.

Office City	Sales Rank	Production Materials Produced	Rank for Production	Damaged Materials	Employees	Percent of Profit	Sales Points	Weeks Without Injuries
Springfield	13.6	271	12	1	34	35	36	7
Philadelphia	17	274	4	3	25	41	20	4
Gary	16	260	10	5	34	34	21	3
Boulder	5	10	6	9	38	15	20	8
Miami	81	3	81	77	133	4	2	0
Houston	2	370	2	0	95	66	100	16
Battle Creek	82	290	82	81	91	13	9	2

13. Between Philadelphia and Battle Creek, how many damaged materials were there? 13.____
A. 84 B. 78 C. 45 D. 86

14. How many offices have had 5 or more weeks without injuries? 14.____
A. 3 B. 4 C. 2 D. 0

15. What was the TOTAL number of damaged materials for the offices in Boulder, Miami, Houston, and Springfield offices? 15.____
A. 91 B. 87 C. 80 D. 77

16. What were the TOTAL sales points of Houston, Battle Creek, and Gary? 16.____
A. 115 B. 145 C. 160 D. 130

17. Which of the offices had the LOWEST number of weeks without an injury? 17.____
A. Battle Creek B. Miami C. Gary D. Philadelphia

18. If worker efficiency is a percentage based on the number of workers at an office and the amount of materials produced, which office has the GREATEST worker efficiency? 18.____
A. Philadelphia B. Springfield C. Boulder D. Gary

19. If the company was looking to close a facility, which of the following factors would NOT be a reason to close the Miami office? 19.____
A. Weeks without injury B. Sales rank
C. Production materials produced D. Employees

Questions 20-25.

DIRECTIONS: In answering Questions 20 through 25, select the sentence in which the underlined word is used correctly.

20. 20.____
A. Jon needs to increase his capitol by 30% to invest in my business.
B. The organization is reevaluating it's decision to purchase the building.
C. The office supply store sells computer paper and stationery.
D. The quarterback and running back left there helmets on the bus.

21. 21.____
A. The police sergeant sited me for disorderly conduct and driving without a license.
B. The votes have already been counted.
C. The professor's theory contradicts the principals of Einstein and Newton.
D. Who's glass of water is on the table?

22. 22.____
A. The board of trustees decided to accept the CEO's resignation.
B. Lose hats will help keep your head from hurting.
C. She complemented me on my exquisite dinner tastes.
D. Jamaal offered him some sound advise.

23. A. In class today, Maya lead us in the reciting of the pledge. 23.____
    B. Doctors worry about the affects of drinking red wine right before bed.
    C. The workers used sledge hammers to break up the pavement.
    D. The teacher gave her students wise council.

24. A. This building was formerly the site of one of the city's oldest department stores. 24.____
    B. In his position, Albert must be very discrete in handling confidential information.
    C. He was to tired to continue the race.
    D. Each of his mortgage payments as about evenly divided between principle and interest.

25. A. The police spent several hours at the cite of the accident. 25.____
    B. A majority of the public support capitol punishment.
    C. The magician used mirrors to create a convincing illusion.
    D. The heiress flouted her wealth by wearing expensive jewelry.

KEY (CORRECT ANSWERS)

1.	D	11.	A
2.	B	12.	A
3.	C	13.	A
4.	A	14.	A
5.	A	15.	B
6.	D	16.	D
7.	B	17.	B
8.	C	18.	A
9.	C	19.	D
10.	B	20.	C

21.	B
22.	A
23.	C
24.	A
25.	C

CLERICAL ABILITIES TEST

EXAMINATION SECTION

TEST 1

DIRECTIONS: Each question or incomplete statement is followed by several suggested answers or completions. Select the one that BEST answers the question or completes the statement. *PRINT THE LETTER OF THE CORRECT ANSWER IN THE SPACE AT THE RIGHT.*

Questions 1-10.

DIRECTIONS: Questions 1 through 10 consist of lines of names, dates, and numbers. For each question, you are to choose the option (A, B, C, or D) in Column II which EXACTLY matches the information in Column I. *PRINT THE LETTER OF THE CORRECT ANSWER IN THE SPACE AT THE RIGHT.*

SAMPLE QUESTION

Column I	Column II
Schneider 11/16/75 581932	A. Schneider 11/16/75 518932
	B. Schneider 11/16/75 581932
	C. Schnieder 11/16/75 581932
	D. Shnieder 11/16/75 518932

The correct answer is B. Only Option B shows the name, date, and number exactly as they are in Column I. Option A has a mistake in the number. Option C has a mistake in the name. Option D has a mistake in the name and in the number. Now answer Questions 1 through 10 in the same manner.

	Column I	Column II	
1.	Johnston 12/26/74 659251	A. Johnson 12/23/74 659251	1.____
		B. Johston 12/26/74 659251	
		C. Johnston 12/26/74 695251	
		D. Johnston 12/26/74 659251	
2.	Allison 1/26/75 9939256	A. Allison 1/26/75 9939256	2.____
		B. Alisson 1/26/75 9939256	
		C. Allison 1/26/76 9399256	
		D. Allison 1/26/75 9993356	
3.	Farrell 2/12/75 361251	A. Farell 2/21/75 361251	3.____
		B. Farrell 2/12/75 361251	
		C. Farrell 2/21/75 361251	
		D. Farrell 2/12/75 361151	

4. Guerrero 4/28/72 105689

A. Guererro 4/28/72 105689
B. Guererro 4/28/72 105986
C. Guerrero 4/28/72 105869
D. Guerrero 4/28/72 105689

4.____

5. McDonnell 6/05/73 478215

A. McDonnell 6/15/73 478215
B. McDonnell 6/05/73 478215
C. McDonnell 6/05/73 472815
D. MacDonell 6/05/73 478215

5.____

6. Shepard 3/31/71 075421

A. Sheperd 3/31/71 075421
B. Shepard 3/13/71 075421
C. Shepard 3/31/71 075421
D. Shepard 3/13/71 075241

6.____

7. Russell 4/01/69 031429

A. Russell 4/01/69 031429
B. Russell 4/10/69 034129
C. Russell 4/10/69 031429
D. Russell 4/01/69 034129

7.____

8. Phillips 10/16/68 961042

A. Philipps 10/16/68 961042
B. Phillips 10/16/68 960142
C. Phillips 10/16/68 961042
D. Philipps 10/16/68 916042

8.____

9. Campbell 11/21/72 624856

A. Campbell 11/21/72 624856
B. Campbell 11/21/72 624586
C. Campbell 11/21/72 624686
D. Campbel 11/21/72 624856

9.____

10. Patterson 9/18/71 76199176

A. Patterson 9/18/72 76191976
B. Patterson 9/18/71 76199176
C. Patterson 9/18/72 76199176
D. Patterson 9/18/71 76919176

10.____

Questions 11-15.

DIRECTIONS: Questions 11 through 15 consist of groups of numbers and letters which you are to compare. For each question, you are to choose the option (A, B,C, or D) in Column I which EXACTLY matches the group of numbers and letters given in Column I.

SAMPLE QUESTION

<u>Column I</u>
B92466

<u>Column II</u>
A. B92644
B. B94266
C. A92466
D. B92466

The correct answer is D. Only Option D in Column II shows the group of numbers and letters EXACTLY as it appears in Column I. Now answer Questions 11 through 15 in the same manner.

	Column I	Column II	
11.	925AC5	A. 952CA5 B. 925AC5 C. 952AC5 D. 925CA6	11.____
12.	Y006925	A. Y060925 B. Y006295 C. Y006529 D. Y006925	12.____
13.	J236956	A. J236956 B. J326965 C. J239656 D. J932656	13.____
14.	AB6952	A. AB6952 B. AB9625 C. AB9652 D. AB6925	14.____
15.	X259361	A. X529361 B. X259631 C. X523961 D. X259361	15.____

Questions 16-25.

DIRECTIONS: Each of questions 16 through 25 consists of three lines of code letters and three lines of numbers. The numbers on each line should correspond with the code letters on the same line in accordance with the table below.

Code Letter	S	V	W	A	Q	M	X	E	G	K
Corresponding Number	0	1	2	3	4	5	5	7	8	9

On some of the lines, an error exists in the coding. Compare the letters and numbers in each question carefully. If you find an error or errors on:

only one of the lines in the question, mark your answer A;
any two lines in the question, mark your answer B;
all three lines in the question, mark your answer C;
none of the lines in the question, mark your answer D.

SAMPLE QUESTION

WQGKSXG	2489068
XEKVQMA	6591453
KMAESXV	9527061

In the above sample, the first line is correct since each code letter listed has the correct corresponding number. On the second line, an error exists because code letter E should have the number 7 instead of the number 5. On the third line, an error exists because the code letter A should have the number 3 instead of the number 2. Since there are errors in two of the three lines, the correct answer is B. Now answer Questions 16 through 25 in the same manner.

16.	SWQEKGA	0247983	16.____
	KEAVSXM	9731065	
	SSAXGKQ	0036894	
17.	QAMKMVS	4259510	17.____
	MGGEASX	5897306	
	KSWMKWS	9125920	
18.	WKXQWVE	2964217	18.____
	QKXXQVA	4966413	
	AWMXGVS	3253810	
19.	GMMKASE	8559307	19.____
	AWVSKSW	3210902	
	QAVSVGK	4310189	
20.	XGKQSMK	6894049	20.____
	QSVKEAS	4019730	
	GSMXKMV	8057951	
21.	AEKMWSG	3195208	21.____
	MKQSVQK	5940149	
	XGQAEVW	6843712	
22.	XGMKAVS	6858310	22.____
	SKMAWEQ	0953174	
	GVMEQSA	8167403	
23.	VQSKAVE	1489317	23.____
	WQGKAEM	2489375	
	MEGKAWQ	5689324	
24.	XMQVSKG	6541098	24.____
	QMEKEWS	4579720	
	KMEVGKG	9571983	

25. GKVAMEW 88912572 25.____
AXMVKAE 3651937
KWAGMAV 9238531

Questions 26-35.

DIRECTIONS: Each of Questions 26 through 35 consists of a column of figures. For each question, add the column of figures and choose the correct answer from the four choices given.

26. 26.____
5,665.43
2,356.69
6,447.24
7,239.65

A. 20,698.01
B. 21,709.01
C. 21,718.01
D. 22,609.01

27. 27.____
817,209.55
264,354.29
82,368.76
849,964.89

A. 1,893.977.49
B. 1,989,988.39
C. 2,009,077.39
D. 2,013,897.49

28. 28.____
156,366.89
249,973.23
823,229.49
56,869.45

A. 1,286,439.06
B. 1,287,521.06
C. 1,297,539.06
D. 1,296,421.06

29. 29.____
23,422.15
149,696.24
238,377.53
86,289.79
505,533.63

A. 989,229.34
B. 999,879.34
C. 1,003,330.34
D. 1,023,329.34

30. 2,468,926.70 30.____
656,842.28
49,723.15
832,369.59

A. 3,218,062.72
B. 3,808,092.72
C. 4,007,861.72
D. 4,818,192.72

31. 524,201.52 31.____
7,775,678.51
8,345,299.63
40,628,898.08
31,374,670.07

A. 88,646,647.81
B. 88,646,747.91
C. 88,648,647.91
D. 88,648,747.81

32. 6,824,829.40 32.____
682,482.94
5,542,015.27
775,678.51
7,732,507.25

A. 21,557,513.37
B. 21,567,513.37
C. 22,567,503.37
D. 22,567,513.37

33. 22,109,405.58 33.____
6,097,093.43
5,050,073.99
8,118,050.05
4,313,980.82

A. 45,688,593.87
B. 45,688,603.87
C. 45,689,593.87
D. 45,689,603.87

34. 79,324,114.19 34.____
99,848,129.74
43,331,653.31
41,610,207.14

A. 264,114,104.38
B. 264,114,114.38
C. 265,114,114.38
D. 265,214,104.38

35. 33,729,653.94 35.____
5,959,342.58
26,052,715.47
4,452,669.52
7,079,953.59

A. 76,374,334.10
B. 76,375,334.10
C. 77,274,335.10
D. 77,275,335.10

Questions 36-40.

DIRECTIONS: Each of Questions 36 through 40 consists of a single number in Column I and four options in Column II. For each question, you are to choose the option (A, B, C, or D) in Column II which EXACTLY matches the number in Column I.

SAMPLE QUESTION

Column I	Column II
5965121	A. 5956121
	B. 5965121
	C. 5966121
	D. 5965211

The correct answer is B. Only Option B shows the number EXACTLY as it appears in Column I. Now answer Questions 36 through 40 in the same manner.

	Column I	Column II	
36.	9643242	A. 9643242	36.____
		B. 9462342	
		C. 9642442	
		D. 9463242	
37.	3572477	A. 3752477	37.____
		B. 3725477	
		C. 3572477	
		D. 3574277	
38.	5276101	A. 5267101	38.____
		B. 5726011	
		C. 5271601	
		D. 5276101	
39.	4469329	A. 4496329	39.____
		B. 4469329	
		C. 4496239	
		D. 4469239	

40. 2326308

A. 2236308
B. 2233608
C. 2326308
D. 2323608

40.____

KEY (CORRECT ANSWERS)

1.	D	11.	B	21.	A	31.	D
2.	A	12.	D	22.	C	32.	A
3.	B	13.	A	23.	B	33.	B
4.	D	14.	A	24.	D	34.	A
5.	B	15.	D	25.	A	35.	C
6.	C	16.	D	26.	B	36.	A
7.	A	17.	C	27.	D	37.	C
8.	C	18.	A	28.	A	38.	D
9.	A	19.	D	29.	C	39.	B
10.	B	20.	B	30.	C	40.	C

TEST 2

DIRECTIONS: Each question or incomplete statement is followed by several suggested answers or completions. Select the one that BEST answers the question or completes the statement. *PRINT THE LETTER OF THE CORRECT ANSWER IN THE SPACE AT THE RIGHT.*

Questions 1-5.

DIRECTIONS: Each of Questions 1 through 5 consists of a name and a dollar amount. In each question, the name and dollar amount in Column II should be an EXACT copy of the name and dollar amount in Column I. If there is:
a mistake only in the name, mark your answer A;
a mistake only in the dollar amount, mark your answer B;
a mistake in both the name and the dollar amount, mark your answer C;
no mistake in either the name or the dollar amount, mark your answer D.

SAMPLE QUESTION

Column I	Column II
George Peterson $125.50	George Petersson $125.50

Compare the name and dollar amount in Column II with the name and dollar amount in Column I. The name *Petersson* in Column II is spelled *Peterson* in Column I. The amount is the same in both columns. Since there is a mistake only in the name, the answer to the sample question is A. Now answer Questions 1 through 5 in the same manner.

	Column I	Column II	
1.	Susanne Shultz $3440	Susanne Schultz $3440	1.____
2.	Anibal P. Contrucci $2121.61	Anibel P. Contrucci $2112.61	2.____
3.	Eugenio Mendoza $12.45	Eugenio Mendozza $12.45	3.____
4.	Maurice Gluckstadt $4297	Maurice Gluckstadt $4297	4.____
5.	John Pampellonne $4656.94	John Pammpellonne $4566.94	5.____

Questions 6-11.

DIRECTIONS: Each of Questions 6 through 11 consist of a set of names and addresses, which you are to compare. In each question, the name and addresses in Column II should be an EXACT copy of the name and address in Column I. If there is:

a mistake only in the name, mark your answer A;
a mistake only in the address, mark your answer B;
a mistake in both the name and address, mark your answer C;
no mistake in either the name or address, mark your answer D.

SAMPLE QUESTION

Column I	Column II
Michael Filbert 456 Reade Street New York, N.Y. 10013	Michael Filbert 645 Reade Street New York, N.Y. 10013

Since there is a mistake only in the address (the street number should be 456 instead of 645), the answer to the sample question is B. Now answer Questions 6 through 11 in the same manner.

	Column I	Column II	
6.	Hilda Goettelmann 55 Lenox Rd. Brooklyn, N.Y. 11226	Hilda Goettelman 55 Lenox Ave. Brooklyn, N.Y. 11226	6.____
7.	Arthur Sherman 2522 Batchelder St. Brooklyn, N.Y. 11235	Arthur Sharman 2522 Batcheder St. Brooklyn, N.Y. 11253	7.____
8.	Ralph Barnett 300 West 28 Street New York, New York 10001	Ralph Barnett 300 West 28 Street New York, New York 10001	8.____
9.	George Goodwin 135 Palmer Avenue Staten Island, New York 10302	George Godwin 135 Palmer Avenue Staten Island, New York 10302	9.____
10.	Alonso Ramirez 232 West 79 Street New York, N.Y. 10024	Alonso Ramirez 223 West 79 Street New York, N.Y. 10024	10.____
11.	Cynthia Graham 149-34 83 Street Howard Beach, N.Y. 11414	Cynthia Graham 149-35 83 Street Howard Beach, N.Y. 11414	11.____

Questions 12-20.

DIRECTIONS: Questions 12 through 20 are problems in subtraction. For each question do the subtraction and select your answer from the four choices given.

12. 232,921.85
-179,587.68 12.____

A. 52,433.17
B. 52,434.17
C. 53,334.17
D. 53,343,17

13. 5,531,876.29
-3,897,158.36 13.____

A. 1,634,717.93
B. 1,644,718.93
C. 1,734,717.93
D. 1,7234,718.93

14. 1,482,658.22
-937,925.76 14.____

A. 544,633.46
B. 544,732.46
C. 545,632.46
D. 545,732.46

15. 937,828.17
-259,673.88 15.____

A. 678,154.29
B. 679,154.29
C. 688,155.39
D. 699,155.39

16. 760,412.38
-263,465.95 16.____

A. 496,046.43
B. 496,946.43
C. 496,956.43
D. 497,046.43

17. 3,203,902.26
-2,933,087.96 17.____

A. 260,814.30
B. 269,824.30
C. 270,814.30
D. 270,824.30

18. 1,023,468.71
-934,678.88 18.____

A. 88,780.83
B. 88,789.83
C. 88,880.83
D. 88,889.83

19. 831,549.47
-772,814.78 19.____

A. 58,734.69
B. 58,834.69
C. 59,735.69
D. 59,834.69

20. 6,306,181.74
-3,617,376.99 20.____

A. 2,687,904.99
B. 2,688,904.99
C. 2,689,804.99
D. 2,799,905.99

Questions 21-30.

DIRECTIONS: Each of Questions 21 through 30 consists of three lines of code letters and three lines of numbers. The numbers on each line should correspond with the code letters on the same line in accordance with the table below.

Code Letter	J	U	B	T	Y	D	K	R	L	P
Corresponding Number	0	1	2	3	4	5	5	7	8	9

On some of the lines, an error exists in the coding. Compare the letters and numbers in each question carefully. If you find an error or errors on:
only *one* of the lines in the question, mark your answer A;
any *two* lines in the question, mark your answer B;
all *three* lines in the question, mark your answer C;
none of the lines in the question, mark your answer D.

SAMPLE QUESTION

BJRPYUR 2079417
DTBPYKJ 5328460
YKLDBLT 4685283

In the above sample, the first line is correct since each code letter listed has the correct corresponding number. On the second line, an error exists because code letter P should have the number 9 instead of the number 8. The third line is correct since each code letter listed has the correct corresponding number. Since there is an error in *one* of the three lines, the correct answer is A. Now answer Questions 21 through 30 in the same manner.

21. BYPDTJL 2495308 21.____
PLRDTJU 9815301
DTJRYLK 5207486

22. RPBYRJK 7934706 22.____
PKTYLBU 9624821
KDLPJYR 6489047

23.	TPYBUJR	3942107	23.____
	BYRKPTU	2476931	
	DUKPYDL	5169458	
24.	KBYDLPL	6345898	24.____
	BLRKBRU	2876261	
	JTULDYB	0318542	
25.	LDPYDKR	8594567	25.____
	BDKDRJL	2565708	
	BDRPLUJ	2679810	
26.	PLRLBPU	9858291	26.____
	LPYKRDJ	88936750	
	TDKPDTR	3569527	
27.	RKURPBY	7617924	27.____
	RYUKPTJ	7426930	
	RTKPTJD	7369305	
28.	DYKPBJT	5469203	28.____
	KLPJBTL	6890238	
	TKPLBJP	3698209	
29.	BTPRJYL	2397148	29.____
	LDKUTYR	8561347	
	YDBLRPJ	4528190	
30.	ULPBKYT	1892643	30.____
	KPDTRBJ	6953720	
	YLKJPTB	4860932	

KEY (CORRECT ANSWERS)

1.	A	11.	D	21.	B
2.	C	12.	C	22.	C
3.	A	13.	A	23.	D
4.	D	14.	B	24.	B
5.	C	15.	A	25.	A
6.	C	16.	B	26.	C
7.	C	17.	C	27.	A
8.	D	18.	B	28.	D
9.	A	19.	A	29.	B
10.	B	20.	B	30.	D

PREPARING WRITTEN MATERIAL

EXAMINATION SECTION

TEST 1

DIRECTIONS: Each of the sentences in this test may be classified under one of the following four categories:

A. *Incorrect* because of faulty grammar or sentence structure
B. *Incorrect* because of faulty punctuation
C. *Incorrect* because of faulty capitalization
D. *Correct*

Examine each sentence carefully to determine under which of the above four options it is best classified. Then, in the space at the right, print the capital letter preceding the option which is the BEST of the four suggested above.

(Each incorrect sentence contains but one type of error. Consider a sentence to be correct if it contains none of the types of errors mentioned, even though there may be other correct ways of expressing the same thought.)

1. This fact, together with those brought out at the previous meeting, prove that the schedule is satisfactory to the employees. 1.____

2. Like many employees in scientific fields, the work of bookkeepers and accountants requires accuracy and neatness. 2.____

3. "What can I do for you," the secretary asked as she motioned to the visitor to take a seat. 3.____

4. Our representative, Mr. Charles will call on you next week to determine whether or not your claim has merit. 4.____

5. We expect you to return in the spring; please do not disappoint us. 5.____

6. Any supervisor, who disregards the just complaints of his subordinates, is remiss in the performance of his duty. 6.____

7. Because she took less than an hour for lunch is no reason for permitting her to leave before five o'clock. 7.____

8. "Miss Smith," said the supervisor, "Please arrange a meeting of the staff for two o'clock on Monday." 8.____

9. A private company's vacation and sick leave allowance usually differs considerably from a public agency. 9.____

10. Therefore, in order to increase the efficiency of operations in the department, a report on the recommended changes in procedures was presented to the departmental committee in charge of the program. 10.____

11. We told him to assign the work to whoever was available. 11.____

12. Since John was the most efficient of any other employee in the bureau, he received the highest service rating. 12.____

13. Only those members of the national organization who resided in the middle West attended the conference in Chicago. 13.____

14. The question of whether the office manager has as yet attained, or indeed can ever hope to secure professional status is one which has been discussed for years. 14.____

15. No one knew who to blame for the error which, we later discovered, resulted in a considerable loss of time. 15.____

KEY (CORRECT ANSWERS)

1.	A	6.	B	11.	D
2.	A	7.	A	12.	A
3.	B	8.	C	13.	C
4.	B	9.	A	14.	B
5.	D	10.	D	15.	A

TEST 2

DIRECTIONS: Each of the sentences in this test may be classified under one of the following four categories:

A. *Incorrect* because of faulty grammar or sentence structure
B. *Incorrect* because of faulty punctuation
C. *Incorrect* because of faulty capitalization
D. *Correct*

1. The National alliance of Businessmen is trying to persuade private businesses to hire youth in the summertime. 1.____

2. The supervisor who is on vacation, is in charge of processing vouchers. 2.____

3. The activity of the committee at its conferences is always stimulating. 3.____

4. After checking the addresses again, the letters went to the mailroom. 4.____

5. The director, as well as the employees, are interested in sharing the dividends. 5.____

KEY (CORRECT ANSWERS)

1. C
2. B
3. D
4. A
5. A

TEST 3

DIRECTIONS: In each of the following groups of sentences, one of the four sentences is faulty in grammar, punctuation, or capitalization. Select the INCORRECT sentence in each case.

1. A. Sailing down the bay was a thrilling experience for me. 1.____
   B. He was not consulted about your joining the club.
   C. This story is different than the one I told you yesterday.
   D. There is no doubt about his being the best player.

2. A. He maintains there is but one road to world peace. 2.____
   B. It is common knowledge that a child sees much he is not supposed to see.
   C. Much of the bitterness might have been avoided if arbitration had been resorted to earlier in the meeting.
   D. The man decided it would be advisable to marry a girl somewhat younger than him.

3. A. In this book, the incident I liked least is where the hero tries to put out the forest fire. 3.____
   B. Learning a foreign language will undoubtedly give a person a better understanding of his mother tongue.
   C. His actions made us wonder what he planned to do next.
   D. Because of the war, we were unable to travel during the summer vacation.

4. A. The class had no sooner become interested in the lesson than the dismissal bell rang. 4.____
   B. There is little agreement about the kind of world to be planned at the peace conference.
   C. "Today," said the teacher, "we shall read 'The Wind in the Willows,' I am sure you'll like it.
   D. The terms of the legal settlement of the family quarrel handicapped both sides for many years.

5. A. I was so surprised that I was not able to say a word. 5.____
   B. She is taller than any other member of the class.
   C. It would be much more preferable if you were never seen in his company.
   D. We had no choice but to excuse her for being late.

KEY (CORRECT ANSWERS)

1. C
2. D
3. A
4. C
5. C

TEST 4

DIRECTIONS: In each of the following groups of sentences, one of the four sentences is faulty in grammar, punctuation, or capitalization. Select the INCORRECT sentence in each case.

1. A. Please send me these data at the earliest opportunity. 1.____
   B. The loss of their material proved to be a severe handicap.
   C. My principal objection to this plan is that it is impracticable.
   D. The doll had laid in the rain for an hour and was ruined.

2. A. The garden scissors, left out all night in the rain, were in a badly rusted condition. 2.____
   B. The girls felt bad about the misunderstanding which had arisen
   C. Sitting near the campfire, the old man told John and I about many exciting adventures he had had.
   D. Neither of us is in a position to undertake a task of that magnitude.

3. A. The general concluded that one of the three roads would lead to the besieged city. 3.____
   B. The children didn't, as a rule, do hardly anything beyond what they were told to do.
   C. The reason the girl gave for her negligence was that she had acted on the spur of the moment.
   D. The daffodils and tulips look beautiful in that blue vase.

4. A. If I was ten years older, I should be interested in this work. 4.____
   B. Give the prize to whoever has drawn the best picture.
   C. When you have finished reading the book, take it back to the library.
   D. My drawing is as good as or better than yours.

5. A. He asked me whether the substance was animal or vegetable. 5.____
   B. An apple which is unripe should not be eaten by a child.
   C. That was an insult to me who am your friend.
   D. Some spy must of reported the matter to the enemy.

6. A. Limited time makes quoting the entire message impossible. 6.____
   B. Who did she say was going?
   C. The girls in your class have dressed more dolls this year than we.
   D. There was such a large amount of books on the floor that I couldn't find a place for my rocking chair.

7. A. What with his sleeplessness and his ill health, he was unable to assume any responsibility for the success of the meeting. 7.____
   B. If I had been born in February, I should be celebrating my birthday soon.
   C. In order to prevent breakage, she placed a sheet of paper between each of the plates when she packed them.
   D. After the spring shower, the violets smelled very sweet.

8. A. He had laid the book down very reluctantly before the end of the lesson. 8.____
B. The dog, I am sorry to say, had lain on the bed all night.
C. The cloth was first lain on a flat surface; then it was pressed with a hot iron.
D. While we were in Florida, we lay in the sun until we were noticeably tanned.

9. A. If John was in New York during the recent holiday season, I have no doubt he spent most of the time with his parents. 9.____
B. How could he enjoy the television program; the dog was barking and the baby was crying.
C. When the problem was explained to the class, he must have been asleep.
D. She wished that her new dress were finished so that she could go to the party.

10. A. The engine not only furnishes power but light and heat as well. 10.____
B. You're aware that we've forgotten whose guilt was established, aren't you?
C. Everybody knows that the woman made many sacrifices for her children.
D. A man with his dog and gun is a familiar sight in this neighborhood.

KEY (CORRECT ANSWERS)

1.	D	6.	D
2.	C	7.	B
3.	B	8.	C
4.	A	9.	B
5.	D	10.	A

TEST 5

DIRECTIONS: Each of Questions 1 through 5 consists of a sentence which may be classified appropriately under one of the following four categories:

A. *Incorrect* because of faulty grammar
B. *Incorrect* because of faulty punctuation
C. *Incorrect* because of faulty spelling
D. *Correct*

Examine each sentence carefully. Then, print in the space at the right the letter preceding the category which is the BEST of the four suggested above

(Note: Each incorrect sentence contains only one type of error. Consider a sentence correct if it contains no errors, although there may be other correct ways of writing the sentence.)

1. Of the two employees, the one in our office is the most efficient. 1.____

2. No one can apply or even understand, the new rules and regulations. 2.____

3. A large amount of supplies were stored in the empty office. 3.____

4. If an employee is occassionally asked to work overtime, he should do so willingly. 4.____

5. It is true that the new procedures are difficult to use but, we are certain that you will learn them quickly. 5.____

6. The office manager said that he did not know who would be given a large allotment under the new plan. 6.____

7. It was at the supervisor's request that the clerk agreed to postpone his vacation. 7.____

8. We do not believe that it is necessary for both he and the clerk to attend the conference. 8.____

9. All employees, who display perseverance, will be given adequate recognition. 9.____

10. He regrets that some of us employees are dissatisfied with our new assignments. 10.____

11. "Do you think that the raise was merited," asked the supervisor? 11.____

12. The new manual of procedure is a valuable supplament to our rules and regulations. 12.____

13. The typist admitted that she had attempted to pursuade the other employees to assist her in her work. 13.____

14. The supervisor asked that all amendments to the regulations be handled by you and I. 14.____

15. The custodian seen the boy who broke the window. 15.____

KEY (CORRECT ANSWERS)

1.	A	6.	D	11.	B
2.	B	7.	D	12.	C
3.	A	8.	A	13.	C
4.	C	9.	B	14.	A
5.	B	10.	D	15.	A

EXAMINATION SECTION

TEST 1

DIRECTIONS: Each question or incomplete statement is followed by several suggested answers or completions. Select the one that BEST answers the question or completes the statement. *PRINT THE LETTER OF THE CORRECT ANSWER IN THE SPACE AT THE RIGHT.*

1. Which of the following sentences is punctuated INCORRECTLY? 1.____
   A. Johnson said, “One tiny virus, Blanche, can multiply so fast that it will become 200 viruses in 25 minutes.”
   B. With economic pressures hitting them from all sides, American farmers have become the weak link in the food chain.
   C. The degree to which this is true, of course, depends on the personalities of the people involved, the subject matter, and the atmosphere in general.
   D. “What loneliness, asked George Eliot, is more lonely than distrust?”

2. Which of the following sentences is punctuated INCORRECTLY? 2.____
   A. Based on past experiences, do you expect the plumber to show up late, not have the right parts, and overcharge you.
   B. When polled, however, the participants were most concerned that it be convenient.
   C. No one mentioned the flavor of the coffee, and no one seemed to care that china was used instead of plastic.
   D. As we said before, sometimes people view others as things; they don’t see them as living, breathing beings like themselves.

3. Convention members travelled here from Kingston New York Pittsfield Massachusetts Bennington Vermont and Hartford Connecticut. 3.____
   How many commas should there be in the above sentence?
   A. 3 B. 4 C. 5 D. 6

4. Of the two speakers the one who spoke about human rights is more famous and more humble. 4.____
   How many commas should there be in the above sentence?
   A. 1 B. 2 C. 3 D. 4

5. Which sentence is punctuated INCORRECTLY? 5.____
   A. Five people voted no; two voted yes; one person abstained.
   B. Well, consider what has been said here today, but we won’t make any promises.
   C. Anthropologists divide history into three major periods: the Stone Age, the Bronze Age, and the Iron Age.
   D. Therefore, we may create a stereotype about people who are unsuccessful; we may see them as lazy, unintelligent, or afraid of success.

6. Which sentence is punctuated INCORRECTLY? 6.____
   A. Studies have found that the unpredictability of customer behavior can lead to a great deal of stress, particularly if the behavior is unpleasant or if the employee has little control over it.
   B. If this degree of emotion and variation can occur in spectator sports, imagine the role that perceptions can play when there are real stakes involved.
   C. At other times, however hidden expectations may sabotage or severely damage an encounter without anyone knowing what happened.
   D. There are usually four issues to look for in a conflict: differences in values, goals, methods, and facts.

Questions 7-10.

DIRECTIONS: Questions 7 through 10 test your ability to distinguish between words that sound alike but are spelled differently and have different meanings. In the following groups of sentences, one of the underlined words is used incorrectly.

7. A. By accepting responsibility for their actions, managers promote trust. 7.____
   B. Dropping hints or making illusions to things that you would like changed sometimes leads to resentment.
   C. The entire unit loses respect for the manager and resents the reprimand.
   D. Many people are averse to confronting problems directly; they would rather avoid them.

8. A. What does this say about the effect our expectations have on those we supervise? 8.____
   B. In an effort to save time between 9 A.M. and 1 P.M., the staff members devised their own interpretation of what was to be done on these forms.
   C. The taskmaster's principal concern is for getting the work done; he or she is not concerned about the need or interests of employees.
   D. The advisor's main objective was increasing Angela's ability to invest her capitol wisely.

9. A. A typical problem is that people have to cope with the internal censer of their feelings. 9.____
   B. Sometimes, in their attempt to sound more learned, people speak in ways that are barely comprehensible.
   C. The council will meet next Friday to decide whether Abrams should continue as representative.
   D. His descent from grace was assured by that final word.

10. A. The doctor said that John's leg had to remain stationary or it would not heal properly. 10.____
   B. There is a city ordinance against parking too close to fire hydrants.
   C. Meyer's problem is that he is never discrete when talking about office politics.
   D. Mrs. Thatcher probably worked harder than any other British Prime Minister had ever worked.

Questions 11-20.

DIRECTIONS: For each of the following groups of sentences in Questions 11 through 20, select the sentence which is the BEST example of English usage and grammar.

11. A. She is a woman who, at age sixty, is distinctly attractive and cares about how they look. 11.____
    B. It was a seemingly impossible search, and no one knew the problems better than she.
    C. On the surface, they are all sweetness and light, but his morbid character is under it.
    D. The minicopier, designed to appeal to those who do business on the run like architects in the field or business travelers, weigh about four pounds.

12. A. Neither the administrators nor the union representative regret the decision to settle the disagreement. 12.____
    B. The plans which are made earlier this year were no longer being considered.
    C. I would have rode with him if I had known he was leaving at five.
    D. I don't know who she said had it.

13. A. Writing at a desk, the memo was handed to her for immediate attention. 13.____
    B. Carla didn't water Carl's plants this week, which she never does.
    C. Not only are they good workers, with excellent writing and speaking skills, and they get to the crux of any problem we hand them.
    D. We've noticed that this enthusiasm for undertaking new projects sometimes interferes with his attention to detail.

14. A. It's obvious that Nick offends people by being unruly, inattentive, and having no patience. 14.____
    B. Marcia told Genie that she would have to leave soon.
    C. Here are the papers you need to complete your investigation.
    D. Julio was startled by you're comment.

15. A. The new manager has done good since receiving her promotion, but her secretary has helped her a great deal. 15.____
    B. One of the personnel managers approached John and tells him that the client arrived unexpectedly.
    C. If somebody can supply us with the correct figures, they should do so immediately.
    D. Like zealots, advocates seek power because they want to influence the policies and actions of an organization.

16. A. Between you and me, Chris probably won't finish this assignment in time. 16.___
    B. Rounding the corner, the snack bar appeared before us.
    C. Parker's radical reputation made to the Supreme Court his appointment impossible.
    D. By the time we arrived, Marion finishes briefing James and returns to Hank's office.

17. A. As we pointed out earlier, the critical determinant of the success of middle managers is their ability to communicate well with others. 17.___
    B. The lecturer stated there wasn't no reason for bad supervision.
    C. We are well aware whose at fault in this instance.
    D. When planning important changes, it's often wise to seek the participation of others because employees often have much valuable ideas to offer.

18. A. Joan had ought to throw out those old things that were damaged when the roof leaked. 18.___
    B. I spose he'll let us know what he's decided when he finally comes to a decision.
    C. Carmen was walking to work when she suddenly realized that she had left her lunch on the table as she passed the market.
    D. Are these enough plants for your new office?

19. A. First move the lever forward, and then they should lift the ribbon casing before trying to take it out. 19.___
    B. Michael finished quickest than any other person in the office.
    C. There is a special meeting for we committee members today at 4 p.m.
    D. My husband is worried about our having to work overtime next week.

20. A. Another source of conflicts are individuals who possess very poor interpersonal skills. 20.___
    B. It is difficult for us to work with him on projects because these kinds of people are not interested in team building.
    C. Each of the departments was represented at the meeting.
    D. Poor boy, he never should of past that truck on the right.

Questions 21-28.

DIRECTIONS: In Questions 21 through 28, there may be a problem with English grammar or usage. If a problem does exist, select the letter that indicates the most effective change. If no problem exists, select Choice A.

21. He rushed her to the hospital and stayed with her, even though this took quite a bit of his time, he didn't charge her anything. 21.___
    A. No changes are necessary.
    B. Change <u>even though</u> to <u>although</u>
    C. Change the first comma to a period and capitalize <u>even</u>
    D. Change <u>rushed</u> to <u>had rushed</u>

22. Waiting that appears unfairly feels longer than waiting that seems justified. 22.____
   A. No changes are necessary.
   B. Change unfairly to unfair
   C. Change appears to seems
   D. Change longer to longest

23. May be you and the person who argued with you will be able to reach an agreement. 23.____
   A. No changes are necessary
   B. Change will be to were
   C. Change argued with to had an argument with
   D. Change May be to Maybe

24. Any one of them could of taken the file while you were having coffee. 24.____
   A. No changes are necessary
   B. Change any one to anyone
   C. Change of to have
   D. Change were having to were out having

25. While people get jobs or move from poverty level to better paying employment, they stop receiving benefits and start paying taxes. 25.____
   A. No changes are necessary
   B. Change While to As
   C. Change stop to will stop
   D. Change get to obtain

26. Maribeth's phone rang while talking to George about the possibility of their meeting Tom at three this afternoon. 26.____
   A. No changes are necessary
   B. Change their to her
   C. Move to George so that it follows Tom
   D. Change talking to she was talking

27. According to their father, Lisa is smarter than Chris, but Emily is the smartest of the three sisters. 27.____
   A. No changes are necessary
   B. Change their to her
   C. Change is to was
   D. Make two sentences, changing the second comma to a period and omitting but

28. Yesterday, Mark and he claim that Carl took Carol's ideas and used them inappropriately. 28.____
   A. No changes are necessary
   B. Change claim to claimed
   C. Change inappropriately to inappropriate
   D. Change Carol's to Carols'

Questions 29-34.

DIRECTIONS: For each group of sentences in Questions 29 through 34, select the choice that represents the BEST editing of the problem sentence.

29. The managers expected employees to be at their desks at all times, but they would always be late or leave unannounced. 29.____
   A. The managers wanted employees to always be at their desks, but they would always be late or leave unannounced.
   B. Although the managers expected employees to be at their desks no matter what came up, they would always be late and leave without telling anyone.
   C. Although the managers expected employees to be at their desks at all times, the managers would always be late or leave without telling anyone.
   D. The managers expected the employee to never leave their desks, but they would always be late or leave without telling anyone.

30. The one who is department manager he will call you to discuss the problem tomorrow morning at 10 A.M. 30.____
   A. The one who is department manager will call you tomorrow morning at ten to discuss the problem.
   B. The department manager will call you to discuss the problem tomorrow at 10 A.M.
   C. Tomorrow morning at 10 A.M., the department manager will call you to discuss the problem.
   D. Tomorrow morning the department manager will call you to discuss the problem.

31. A conference on child care in the workplace the $200 cost of which to attend may be prohibitive to childcare workers who earn less than that weekly. 31.____
   A. A conference on child care in the workplace that costs $200 may be too expensive for childcare workers who earn less than that each week.
   B. A conference on child care in the workplace, the cost of which to attend is $200, may be prohibitive to childcare workers who earn less than that weekly.
   C. A conference on child care in the workplace who costs $200 may be too expensive for childcare workers who earn less than that a week.
   D. A conference on child care in the workplace which costs $200 may be too expensive to childcare workers who earn less than that on a weekly basis.

32. In accordance with estimates recently made, there are 40,000 to 50,000 nuclear weapons in our world today. 32.____
   A. Because of estimates recently, there are 40,000 to 50,000 nuclear weapons in the world today.
   B. In accordance with estimates made recently, there are 40,000 to 50,000 nuclear weapons in the world today.

C. According to estimates made recently, there are 40,000 to 50,000 weapons in the world today.
D. According to recent estimates, there are 40,000 to 50,000 nuclear weapons in the world today.

33. Motivation is important in problem solving, but they say that excessive motivation can inhibit the creative process. 33.____
A. Motivation is important in problem solving, but, as they say, too much of it can inhibit the creative process.
B. Motivation is important in problem solving and excessive motivation will inhibit the creative process.
C. Motivation is important in problem solving, but excessive motivation can inhibit the creative process.
D. Motivation is important in problem solving because excessive motivation can inhibit the creative process.

34. In selecting the best option calls for consulting with all the people that are involved in it. 34.____
A. In selecting the best option consulting with all people concerned with it.
B. Calling for the best option, we consulted all the affected people.
C. We called all the people involved to select the best option.
D. To be sure of selecting the best option, one should consult all the people involved.

35. There are a number of problems with the following letter. From the options below, select the version that is MOST in accordance with standard business style, tone, and form. 35.____

Dear Sir:

We are so sorry that we have had to backorder your order for 15,000 widgets and 2,300 whatzits for such a long time. We have been having incredibly bad luck lately. When your order first came in no one could get to it because my secretary was out with the flu and her replacement didn't know what she was doing, then there was the dock strike in Cucamonga which held things up for awhile, and then it just somehow got lost. We think it may have fallen behind the radiator.

We are happy to say that all these problems have been taken care of, we are caught up on supplies, and we should have the stuff to you soon, in the near future—about two weeks. You may not believe us after everything you've been through with us, but it's true.

We'll let you know as soon as we have a secure date for delivery. Thank you so much for continuing to do business with us after all the problems this probably has caused you.

Yours very sincerely,
Rob Barker

A. Dear Sir:

We are so sorry that we have had to backorder your order for 15,000 widgets and 2,300 whatzits. We have been having problems with staff lately and the dock strike hasn't helped anything.

We are happy to say that all these problems have been taken care of. I've told my secretary to get right on it, and we should have the stuff to you soon. Thank you so much for continuing to do business with us after all the problems this must have caused you.

We'll let you know as soon as we have a secure date for delivery.

Sincerely,
Rob Barker

B. Dear Sir:

We regret that we haven't been able to fill your order for 15,000 widgets and 2,300 whatzits in a timely fashion.

We'll let you know as soon as we have a secure date for delivery.

Sincerely,
Rob Barker

C. Dear Sir:

We are so very sorry that we haven't been able to fill your order for 15,000 widgets and 2,300 whatzits. We have been having incredibly bad luck lately, but things are much better now.

Thank you so much for bearing with us through all of this. We'll let you know as soon as we have a secure date for delivery.

Sincerely,
Rob Barker

D. Dear Sir:

We are very sorry that we haven't been able to fill your order for 15,000 widgets and 2,300 whatzits. Due to unforeseen difficulties, we have had to back-order your request. At this time, supplies have caught up to demand, and we foresee a delivery date within the next two weeks.

We'll let you know as soon as we have a secure date for delivery. Thank you for your patience.

Sincerely,
Rob Barker

KEY (CORRECT ANSWERS)

1.	D	11.	B	21.	C	31.	A
2.	A	12.	D	22.	B	32.	D
3.	B	13.	D	23.	D	33.	C
4.	A	14.	C	24.	C	34.	D
5.	B	15.	D	25.	B	35.	D
6.	C	16.	A	26.	D		
7.	B	17.	A	27.	A		
8.	D	18.	D	28.	B		
9.	A	19.	D	29.	C		
10.	C	20.	C	30.	B		

EXAMINATION SECTION

TEST 1

DIRECTIONS: In each of the following questions, only one of the four sentences conforms to standards of correct usage. The other three contain errors in grammar, diction, or punctuation. Select the choice in each question which BEST conforms to standards of correct usage. Consider a choice correct if it contains none of the errors mentioned above, even though there may be other ways of expressing the same thought. *PRINT THE LETTER OF THE CORRECT ANSWER IN THE SPACE AT THE RIGHT.*

1. A. Because he was ill was no excuse for his behavior 1.____
   B. In insist that he see a lawyer before he goes to trial.
   C. He said "that he had not intended to go."
   D. He wasn't out of the office only three days.

2. A. He came to the station and pays a porter to carry his bags into the train. 2.____
   B. I should have liked to live in medieval times.
   C. My father was born in Linville. A little country town where everybody knows everyone else.
   D. The car, which is parked across the street, is disabled.

3. A. He asked the desk clerk for a clean, quiet, room. 3.____
   B. I expected James to be lonesome and that he would want to go home.
   C. I have stopped worrying because I have heard nothing further on the subject.
   D. If the board of directors controls the company, they may take actions which are disapproved by the stockholders.

4. A. Each of the players knew their place. 4.____
   B. He whom you saw on the stage is the son of an actor.
   C. Susan is the smartest of the twin sisters.
   D. Who ever thought of him winning both prizes?

5. A. An outstanding trait of early man was their reliance on omens. 5.____
   B. Because I had never been there before.
   C. Neither Mr. Jones nor Mr. Smith has completed his work.
   D. While eating my dinner, a dog came to the window.

6. A. A copy of the lease, in addition to the Rules and Regulations, are to be given to each tenant. 6.____
   B. The Rules and Regulations and a copy of the lease is being given to each tenant.
   C. A copy of the lease, in addition to the Rules and Regulations, is to be given to each tenant.
   D. A copy of the lease, in addition to the Rules and Regulations, are being given to each tenant.

7. A. Although we understood that for him music was a passion, we were disturbed by the fact that he was addicted to sing along with the soloists. 7.____
   B. Do you believe that Steven is liable to win a scholarship?
   C. Give the picture to whomever is a connoisseur of art.
   D. Whom do you believe to be the most efficient worker in the office?

8. A. Each adult who is sure they know all the answers will some day realize their mistake. 8.____
   B. Even the most hardhearted villain would have to feel bad about so horrible a tragedy.
   C. Neither being licensed teachers, both aspirants had to pass rigorous tests before being appointed.
   D. The principal reason why he wanted to be designated was because he had never before been to a convention.

9. A. Being that the weather was so inclement, the party has been postponed for at least a month. 9.____
   B. He is in New York City only three weeks and he has already seen all the thrilling sights in Manhattan and in the other four boroughs.
   C. If you will look it up in the official directory, which can be consulted in the library during specified hours, you will discover that the chairman and director are Mr. T. Henry Long.
   D. Working hard at college during the day and at the post office during the night, he appeared to his family to be indefatigable.

10. A. I would have been happy to oblige you if you only asked me to do it. 10.____
    B. The cold weather, as well as the unceasing wind and rain, have made us decide to spend the winter in Florida.
    C. The politician would have been more successful in winning office if he would have been less dogmatic.
    D. These trousers are expensive; however, they will wear well.

11. A. All except him wore formal attire at the reception for the ambassador. 11.____
    B. If that chair were to be blown off of the balcony, it might injure someone below.
    C. Not a passenger, who was in the crash, survived the impact.
    D. To borrow money off friends is the best way to lose them.

12. A. Approaching Manhattan on the ferry boat from Staten Island, an unforgettable sight of the skyscrapers is seen. 12.____
    B. Did you see the exhibit of modernistic paintings as yet?
    C. Gesticulating wildly and ranting in stentorian tones, the speaker was the sinecure of all eyes.
    D. The airplane with crew and passengers was lost somewhere in the Pacific Ocean.

13. A. If one has consistently had that kind of training, it is certainly too late to change your entire method of swimming long distances. 13.____
    B. The captain would have been more impressed if you would have been more conscientious in evacuation drills.
    C. The passengers on the stricken ship were all ready to abandon it at the signal.
    D. The villainous shark lashed at the lifeboat with it's tail, trying to upset the rocking boat in order to partake of it's contents.

14. A. As one whose been certified as a professional engineer, I believe that the decision to build a bridge over that harbor is unsound. 14.____
    B. Between you and me, this project ought to be completed long before winter arrives.
    C. He fervently hoped that the men would be back at camp and to find them busy at their usual chores.
    D. Much to his surprise, he discovered that the climate of Korea was like his home town.

15. A. An industrious executive is aided, not impeded, by having a hobby which gives him a fresh point of view on life and its problems. 15.____
    B. Frequent absence during the calendar year will surely mitigate against the chances of promotion.
    C. He was unable to go to the committee meeting because he was very ill.
    D. Mr. Brown expressed his disapproval so emphatically that his associates were embarassed

16. A. At our next session, the office manager will have told you something about his duties and responsibilities. 16.____
    B. In general, the book is absorbing and original and have no hesitation about recommending it.
    C. The procedures followed by private industry in dealing with lateness and absence are different from ours.
    D We shall treat confidentially any information about Mr. Doe, to whom we understand you have sent reports to for many years.

17. A. I talked to one official, whom I knew was fully impartial. 17.____
    B. Everyone signed the petition but him.
    C. He proved not only to be a good student but also a good athlete.
    D. All are incorrect.

18. A. Every year a large amount of tenants are admitted to housing projects. 18.____
    B. Henry Ford owned around a billion dollars in industrial equipment.
    C. He was aggravated by the child's poor behavior.
    D. All are incorrect.

19. A. Before he was committed to the asylum he suffered from the illusion that he was Napoleon. 19.____
    B. Besides stocks, there were also bonds in the safe.
    C. We bet the other team easily.
    D. All are incorrect.

20. A. Bring this report to your supervisory. 20.____
    B. He set the chair down near the table.
    C. The capitol of New York is Albany.
    D. All are incorrect.

21. A. He was chosen to arbitrate the dispute because everyone knew he would be disinterested. 21.____
    B. It is advisable to obtain the best council before making an important decision.
    C. Less college students are interested in teaching than ever before.
    D. All are incorrect.

22. A. She, hearing a signal, the source lamp flashed. 22.____
    B. While hearing a signal, the source lamp flashed.
    C. In hearing a signal, the source lamp flashed.
    D. As she heard a signal, the source lamp flashed.

23. A. Every one of the time records have been initialed in the designated spaces. 23.____
    B. All of the time records has been initialed in the designated spaces.
    C. Each one of the time records was initialed in the designated spaces.
    D. The time records all been initialed in the designated spaces.

24. A. If there is no one else to answer the phone, you will have to answer it. 24.____
    B. You will have to answer it yourself if no one else answers the phone.
    C. If no one else is not around to pick up the phone, you will have to do it.
    D. You will have to answer the phone when nobodys here to do it.

25. A. Dr. Barnes not in his office. What could I do for you? 25.____
    B. Dr. Barnes is not in his office. Is there something I can do for you?
    C. Since Dr. Barnes is not in his office, might there be something I may do for you?
    D. Is there any ways I can assist you since Dr. Barnes is not in his office?

26. A. She do not understand how the new console works. 26.____
    B. The way the new console works, she doesn't understand.
    C. She doesn't understand how the new console works.
    D. The new console works, so that she doesn't understand.

27. A. Certain changes in my family income must be reported as they occur. 27.____
    B. When certain changes in family income occur, it must be reported.
    C. Certain family income change must be reported as they occur.
    D. Certain changes in family income must be reported as they have been occurring.

28. A. Each tenant has to complete the application themselves. 28.____
    B. Each of the tenants have to complete the application by himself.
    C. Each of the tenants has to complete the application himself.
    D. Each of the tenants has to complete the application by themselves.

29. A. Yours is the only building that the construction will effect. 29.____
    B. Your's is the only building affected by the construction.
    C. The construction will only effect your building.
    D. Yours is the only building that will be affected by the construction.

30. A. There is four tests left. 30.____
    B. The number of tests left are four.
    C. There are four tests left.
    D. Four of the tests remains.

31. A. Each of the applicants takes a test. 31.____
    B. Each of the applicant take a test.
    C. Each of the applicants take tests.
    D. Each of the applicants have taken tests.

32. A. The applicant, not the examiners, are ready. 32.____
    B. The applicants, not the examiners, is ready.
    C. The applicants, not the examiner, are ready.
    D. The applicant, not the examiner, are ready

33. A. You will not progress except you practice. 33.____
    B. You will not progress without you practicing.
    C. You will not progress unless you practice.
    D. You will not progress provided you do not practice.

34. A. Neither the director or the employees will be at the office tomorrow. 34.____
    B. Neither the director nor the employees will be at the office tomorrow.
    C. Neither the director, or the secretary nor the other employees will be at the office tomorrow.
    D. Neither the director, the secretary or the other employees will be at the office tomorrow.

35. A. In my absence, he and her will have to finish the assignment. 35.____
    B. In my absence he and she will have to finish the assignment.
    C. In my absence she and him, they will have to finish the assignment.
    D. In my absence he and her both will have to finish the assignment.

KEY (CORRECT ANSWERS)

1.	B	11.	A	21.	A	31.	A
2.	B	12.	D	22.	D	32.	C
3.	C	13.	C	23.	C	33.	C
4.	B	14.	B	24.	A	34.	B
5.	C	15.	A	25.	B	35.	B
6.	C	16.	C	26.	C		
7.	D	17.	B	27.	A		
8.	B	18.	D	28.	C		
9.	D	19.	B	29.	D		
10.	D	20.	B	30.	C		

TEST 2

DIRECTIONS: Each question or incomplete statement is followed by several suggested answers or completions. Select the one that BEST answers the question or completes the statement. *PRINT THE LETTER OF THE CORRECT ANSWER IN THE SPACE AT THE RIGHT.*

Questions 1-4.

DIRECTIONS: Questions 1 through 4 consist of three sentences each. For each question, select the sentence which contains NO error in grammar or usage.

1. A. Be sure that everybody brings his notes to the conference. 1.____
   B. He looked like he meant to hit the boy.
   C. Mr. Jones is one of the clients who was chosen to represent the district.
   D. All are incorrect.

2. A. He is taller than I. 2.____
   B. I'll have nothing to do with these kind of people.
   C. The reason why he will not buy the house is because it is too expensive.
   D. All are incorrect.

3. A. Aren't I eligible for this apartment. 3.____
   B. Have you seen him anywheres?
   C. He should of come earlier.
   D. All are incorrect.

4. A. He graduated college in 1982. 4.____
   B. He hadn't but one more line to write.
   C. Who do you think is the author of this report?
   D. All are incorrect.

Questions 5-35.

DIRECTIONS: In each of the following questions, only one of the four sentences conforms to standards of correct usage. The other three contain errors in grammar, diction, or punctuation. Select the choice in each question which BEST conforms to standards of correct usage. Consider a choice correct if it contains none of the errors mentioned above, even though there may be other ways of expressing the same thought.

5. A. It is obvious that no one wants to be a kill-joy if they can help it. 5.____
   B. It is not always possible, and perhaps it never ispossible, to judge a person's character by just looking at him.
   C. When Yogi Berra of the New York Yankees hit an immortal grandslam home run, everybody in the huge stadium including Pittsburgh fans, rose to his feet.
   D. Every one of us students must pay tuition today.

6. A. The physician told the young mother that if the baby is not able to digest its milk, it should be boiled. 6.____
   B. There is no doubt whatsoever that he felt deeply hurt because John Smith had betrayed the trust.
   C. Having partaken of a most delicious repast prepared by Tessie Breen, the hostess, the horses were driven home immediately thereafter.
   D. The attorney asked my wife and myself several questions.

7. A. Despite all denials, there is no doubt in my mind that 7.____
   B. At this time everyone must deprecate the demogogic attack made by one of our Senators on one of our most revered statesmen.
   C. In the first game of a crucial two-game series, Ted Williams, got two singles, both of them driving in a run.
   D. Our visitor brought good news to John and I.

8. A. If he would have told me, I should have been glad to help him in his dire financial emergency. 8.____
   B. Newspaper men have often asserted that diplomats or so-called official spokesmen sometimes employ equivocation in attempts to deceive.
   C. I think someones coming to collect money for the Red Cross.
   D. In a masterly summation, the young attorney expressed his belief that the facts clearly militate against this opinion.

9. A. We have seen most all the exhibits. 9.____
   B. Without in the least underestimating your advice, in my opinion the situation has grown immeasurably worse in the past few days.
   C. I wrote to the box office treasurer of the hit show that a pair of orchestra seats would be preferable.
   D. As the grim story of Pearl Harbor was broadcast on that fateful December 7, it was the general opinion that war was inevitable.

10. A. Without a moment's hesitation, Casey Stengel said that Larry Berra works harder than any player on the team. 10.____
    B. There is ample evidence to indicate that many animals can run faster than any human being.
    C. No one saw the accident but I.
    D. Example of courage is the heroic defense put up by the paratroopers against overwhelming odds.

11. A. If you prefer these kind, Mrs. Grey, we shall be more than willing to let you have them reasonably. 11.____
    B. If you like these here, Mrs. Grey, we shall be more than willing to let you have them reasonably.
    C. If you like these, Mrs. Grey, we shall be more than willing to let you have them.
    D. Who shall we appoint?

12. A. The number of errors are greater in speech than in writing. 12.____
    B. The doctor rather than the nurse was to blame for his being neglected.
    C. Because the demand for these books have been so great, we reduced the price.
    D. John Galsworthy, the English novelist, could not have survived a serious illness; had it not been for loving care.

13. A. Our activities this year have seldom ever been as interesting as they have been this month. 13.____
    B. Our activities this month have been more interesting, or at least as interesting as those of any month this year.
    C. Our activities this month has been more interesting than those of any other month this year.
    D. Neither Jean nor her sister was at home.

14. A. George B. Shaw's view of common morality, as well as his wit sparkling with a dash of perverse humor here and there, have led critics to term him "The Incurable Rebel." 14.____
    B. The President's program was not always received with the wholehearted endorsement of his own party, which is why the party faces difficulty in drawing up a platform for the coming election.
    C. The reason why they wanted to travel was because they had never been away from home.
    D. Facing a barrage of cameras, the visiting celebrity found it extremely difficult to express his opinions clearly.

15. A. When we calmed down, we all agreed that our anger had been kind of unnecessary and had not helped the situation. 15.____
    B. Without him going into all the details, he made us realize the horror of the accident.
    C. Like one girl, for example, who applied for two positions.
    D. Do not think that you have to be so talented as he is in order to play in the school orchestra.

16. A. He looked very peculiarly to me. 16.____
    B. He certainly looked at me peculiar.
    C. Due to the train's being late, we had to wait an hour.
    D. The reason for the poor attendance is that it is raining.

17. A. About one out of four own an automobile. 17.____
    B. The collapse of the old Mitchell Bridge was caused by defective construction in the central pier.
    C. Brooks Atkinson was well acquainted with the best literature, thus helping him to become an able critic.
    D. He has to stand still until the relief man comes up, thus giving him no chance to move about and keep warm.

18. A. He is sensitive to confusion and withdraws from people whom he feels are too noisy. 18.____
    B. Do you know whether the data is statistically correct?
    C. Neither the mayor or the aldermen are to blame.
    D. Of those who were graduated from high school, a goodly percentage went to college.

19. A. Acting on orders, the offices were searched by a designated committee. 19.____
    B. The answer probably is nothing.
    C. I thought it to be all right to excuse them from class.
    D. I think that he is as successful a singer, if not more successful, than Mary.

20. A. $120,000 is really very little to pay for such a wellbuilt house. 20.____
    B. The creatures looked like they had come from outer space.
    C. It was her, he knew!
    D. Nobody but me knows what to do.

21. A. Mrs. Smith looked good in her new suit. 21.____
    B. New York may be compared with Chicago.
    C. I will not go to the meeting except you go with me.
    D. I agree with this editorial.

22. A. My opinions are different from his. 22.____
    B. There will be less students in class now.
    C. Helen was real glad to find her watch.
    D. It had been pushed off of her dresser.

23. A. Almost everyone, who has been to California, returns with glowing reports. 23.____
    B. George Washington, John Adams, and Thomas Jefferson, were our first presidents.
    C. Mr. Walters, whom we met at the bank yesterday, is the man, who gave me my first job.
    D. One should study his lessons as carefully as he can.

24. A. We had such a good time yesterday. 24.____
    B. When the bell rang, the boys and girls went in the schoolhouse.
    C. John had the worst headache when he got up this morning.
    D. Today's assignment is somewhat longer than yesterday's.

25. A. Neither the mayor nor the city clerk are willing to talk. 25.____
    B. Neither the mayor nor the city clerk is willing to talk.
    C. Neither the mayor or the city clerk are willing to talk.
    D Neither the mayor or the city clerk is willing to talk.

26. A. Being that he is that kind of boy, cooperation cannot be expected. 26.____
    B. He interviewed people who he thought had something to say.
    C. Stop whomever enters the building regardless of rank or office held.
    D. Passing through the countryside, the scenery pleased us.

27. A. The childrens' shoes were in their closet. 27.____
B. The children's shoes were in their closet.
C. The childs' shoes were in their closet.
D. The childs' shoes were in his closet.

28. A. An agreement was reached between the defendant, the plaintiff, the plaintiff's attorney and the insurance company as to the amount of the settlement. 28.____
B. Everybody was asked to give their versions of the accident.
C. The consensus of opinion was that the evidence was inconclusive.
D. The witness stated that if he was rich, he wouldn't have had to loan the money.

29. A. Before beginning the investigation, all the materials related to the case were carefully assembled. 29.____
B. The reason for his inability to keep the appointment is because of his injury in the accident.
C. This here evidence tends to support the claim of the defendant.
D. We interviewed all the witnesses who, according to the driver, were still in town.

30. A. Each claimant was allowed the full amount of their medical expenses. 30.____
B. Either of the three witnesses is available.
C. Every one of the witnesses was asked to tell his story.
D. Neither of the witnesses are right.

31. A. The commissioner, as well as his deputy and various bureau heads, were present. 31.____
B. A new organization of employers and employees have been formed.
C. One or the other of these men have been selected.
D. The number of pages in the book is enough to discourage a reader.

32. A. Between you and me, I think he is the better man. 32.____
B. He was believed to be me.
C. Is it us that you wish to see?
D. The winners are him and her.

33. A. Beside the statement to the police, the witness spoke to no one. 33.____
B. He made no statement other than to the police and I.
C. He made no statement to any one else, aside from the police.
D. The witness spoke to no one but me.

34. A. The claimant has no one to blame but himself. 34.____
B. The boss sent us, he and I, to deliver the packages.
C. The lights come from mine and not his car.
D. There was room on the stairs for him and myself.

35. A. Admission to this clinic is limited to patients' inability to pay for medical care. 35.____
    B. Patients who can pay little or nothing for medical care are treated in this clinic.
    C. The patient's ability to pay for medical care is the determining factor in his admission to this clinic.
    D. This clinic is for the patient's that cannot afford to pay or that can pay a little for medical care.

KEY (CORRECT ANSWERS)

1.	A	11.	C	21.	A	31.	D
2.	A	12.	B	22.	A	32.	A
3.	D	13.	D	23.	D	33.	D
4.	C	14.	D	24.	D	34.	A
5.	D	15.	D	25.	B	35.	B
6.	D	16.	D	26.	B		
7.	B	17.	B	27.	B		
8.	B	18.	D	28.	C		
9.	D	19.	B	29.	D		
10.	B	20.	D	30.	C		

PREPARING WRITTEN MATERIAL

PARAGRAPH REARRANGEMENT COMMENTARY

The sentences that follow are in scrambled order. You are to rearrange them in proper order and indicate the letter choice containing the correct answer at the space at the right.

Each group of sentences in this section is actually a paragraph presented in scrambled order. Each sentence in the group has a place in that paragraph; no sentence is to be left out. You are to read each group of sentences and decide upon the best order in which to put the sentences so as to form a well-organized paragraph.

The questions in this section measure the ability to solve a problem when all the facts relevant to its solution are not given.

More specifically, certain positions of responsibility and authority require the employee to discover connection between events sometimes, apparently, unrelated. In order to do this, the employee will find it necessary to correctly infer that unspecified events have probably occurred or are likely to occur. This ability becomes especially important when action must be taken on incomplete information.

Accordingly, these questions require competitors to choose among several suggested alternatives, each of which presents a different sequential arrangement of the events. Competitors must choose the MOST logical of the suggested sequences.

In order to do so, they may be required to draw on general knowledge to infer missing concepts or events that are essential to sequencing the given events. Competitors should be careful to infer only what is essential to the sequence. The plausibility of the wrong alternatives will always require the inclusion of unlikely events or of additional chains of events which are NOT essential to sequencing the given events.

It's very important to remember that you are looking for the best of the four possible choices, and that the best choice of all may not even be one of the answers you're given to choose from.

There is no one right way to solve these problems. Many people have found it helpful to first write out the order of the sentences, as they would have arranged them, on their scrap paper before looking at the possible answers. If their optimum answer is there, this can save them some time. If it isn't, this method can still give insight into solving the problem. Others find it most helpful to just go through each of the possible choices, contrasting each as they go along. You should use whatever method feels comfortable and works for you.

While most of these types of questions are not that difficult, we've added a higher percentage of the difficult type, just to give you more practice. Usually there are only one or two questions on this section that contain such subtle distinctions that you're unable to answer confidently. And you then may find yourself stuck deciding between two possible choices, neither of which you're sure about.

EXAMINATION SECTION

TEST 1

DIRECTIONS: The following groups of sentences need to be arranged in an order that makes sense. Select the letter preceding the sequence that represents the BEST sentence order. *PRINT THE LETTER OF THE CORRECT ANSWER IN THE SPACE AT THE RIGHT.*

1. I. The keyboard was purposely designed to be a little awkward to slow typists down. 1.____
   II. The arrangement of letters on the keyboard of a typewriter was not designed for the convenience of the typist.
   III. Fortunately, no one is suggesting that a new keyboard be designed right away.
   IV. If one were, we would have to learn to type all over again.
   V. The reason was that the early machines were slower than the typists and would jam easily.
   The CORRECT answer is:
   A. I, III, IV, II, V
   B. II, V, I, IV, III
   C. V, I, II, III, IV
   D. II, I, V, III, IV

2. I. The majority of the new service jobs are part-time or low-paying. 2.____
   II. According to the U.S. Bureau of Labor Statistics, jobs in the service sector constitute 72% of all jobs in this country.
   III. If more and more workers receive less and less money, who will buy the goods and services needed to keep the economy going?
   IV. The service sector is by far the fastest growing part of the United States economy.
   V. Some economists look upon this trend with great concern.
   The CORRECT answer is:
   A. II, IV, I, V, III
   B. II, III, IV, I, V
   C. V, IV, II, III, I
   D. III, I, II, IV, V

3. I. They can also affect one's endurance. 3.____
   II. This can stabilize blood sugar levels, and ensure that the brain is receiving a steady, constant, supply of glucose, so that one is *hitting on all cylinders* while taking the test.
   III. By food, we mean real food, not junk food or unhealthy snacks.
   IV. For this reason, it is important not to skip a meal, and to bring food with you to the exam.
   V. One's blood sugar levels can affect how clearly one is able to think and concentrate during an exam.
   The CORRECT answer is:
   A. V, IV, II, III, I
   B. V, II, I, IV, III
   C. V, I, IV, III, II
   D. V, IV, I, III, II

4. I. Those who are the embodiment of desire are absorbed in material quests, and those who are the embodiment of feeling are warriors who value power more than possession. 4.____
II. These qualities are in everyone, but in different degrees.
III. But those who value understanding yearn not for goods or victory, but for knowledge.
IV. According to Plato, human behavior flows from three main sources: desire, emotion, and knowledge.
V. In the perfect state, the industrial forces would produce but not rule, the military would protect but not rule, and the forces of knowledge, the philosopher kings, would reign.
The CORRECT answer is:
A. IV, V, I, II, III
B. V, I, II, III, IV
C. IV, III, II, I, V
D. IV, II, I, III, V

5. I. Of the more than 26,000 tons of garbage produced daily in New York City, 12,000 tons arrive daily at Fresh Kills. 5.____
II. In a month, enough garbage accumulates there to fill the Empire State Building.
III. In 1937, the Supreme Court halted the practice of dumping the trash of New York City into the sea.
IV. Although the garbage is compacted, in a few years the mounds of garbage at Fresh Kills will be the highest points south of Maine's Mount Desert Island on the Eastern Seaboard.
V. Instead, tugboats now pull barges of much of the trash to Staten Island and the largest landfill in the world, Fresh Kills.
The CORRECT answer is:
A. III, V, IV, I, II
B. III, V, II, IV, I
C. III, V, I, II, IV
D. III, II, V, IV, I

6. I. Communists rank equality very high, but freedom very low. 6.____
II. Unlike communists, conservatives place a high value on freedom and a very low value on equality.
III. A recent study demonstrated that one way to classify people's political beliefs is to look at the importance placed on two words: freedom and equality.
IV. Thus, by demonstrating how members of these groups feel about the two words, the study has proved to be useful for political analysts in several European countries.
V. According to the study, socialists and liberals rank both freedom and equality very high, while fascists rate both very low.
The CORRECT answer is:
A. III, V, I, II, IV
B. V, IV, III, I, II
C. III, V, IV, II, I
D. III, I, II, IV, V

7. I. "Can there be anything more amazing than this?" 7.____
II. If the riddle is successfully answered, his dead brothers will be brought back to life.
III. "Even though man sees those around him dying every day," says Dharmaraj, "he still believes and acts as if he were immortal."
IV. "What is the cause of ceaseless wonder?" asks the Lord of the Lake.
V. In the ancient epic, The Mahabharata, a riddle is asked of one of the Pandava brothers.
The CORRECT answer is:
A. V, II, I, IV, III
B. V, IV, III, I, II
C. V, II, IV, III, I
D. V, II, IV, I, III

8. I. On the contrary, the two main theories—the cooperative (neoclassical) theory and the radical (labor theory)—clearly rest on very different assumptions, which have very different ethical overtones. 8.____
II. The distribution of income is the primary factor in determining the relative levels of material well-being that different groups or individuals attain.
III. Of all issues in economics, the distribution of income is one of the most controversial.
IV. The neoclassical theory tends to support the existing income distribution (or minor changes), while the labor theory ends to support substantial changes in the way income is distributed.
V. The intensity of the controversy reflects the fact that different economic theories are not purely neutral, *detached* theories with no ethical or moral implications.
The CORRECT answer is:
A. II, I, V, IV, III
B. III, II, V, I, IV
C. III, V, II, I, IV
D. III, V, IV, I, II

9. I. The pool acts as a broker and ensures that the cheapest power gets used first. 9.____
II. Every six seconds, the pool's computer monitors all of the generating stations in the state and decides which to ask for more power and which to cut back.
III. The buying and selling of electrical power is handled by the New York Power Pool in Guilderland, New York.
IV. This is to the advantage of both the buying and selling utilities.
V. The pool began operation in 1970, and consists of the state's eight electric utilities.
The CORRECT answer is:
A. V, I, II, III, IV
B. IV, II, I, III, V
C. III, V, I, IV, II
D. V, III, IV, II, I

10. I. Modern English is much simpler grammatically than Old English. 10.____
II. Finnish grammar is very complicated; there are some fifteen cases, for example.
III. Chinese, a very old language, may seem to be the exception, but it is the great number of characters/words that must be mastered that makes it so difficult to learn, not its grammar.
IV. The newest literary language—that is, written as well as spoken—is Finish, whose literary roots go back only to about the middle of the nineteenth century.
V. Contrary to popular belief, the longer a language is been in use the simpler its grammar—not the reverse.

The CORRECT answer is:

A. IV, I, II, III, V
B. V, I, IV, II, III
C. I, II, IV, III, V
D. IV, II, III, I, V

KEY (CORRECT ANSWERS)

1.	D	6.	A
2.	A	7.	C
3.	C	8.	B
4.	D	9.	C
5.	C	10.	B

TEST 2

DIRECTIONS: This type of question tests your ability to recognize accurate paraphrasing, well-constructed paragraphs, and appropriate style and tone. It is important that the answer you select contains only the facts or concepts given in the original sentences. It is also important that you be aware of incomplete sentences, inappropriate transitions, unsupported opinions, incorrect usage, and illogical sentence order. Paragraphs that do not include all the necessary facts and concepts, that distort them, or that add new ones are not considered correct.

The format for this section may vary. Sometimes, long paragraphs are given, and emphasis is placed on style and organization. Our first five questions are of this type. Other times, the paragraphs are shorter, and there is less emphasis on style and more emphasis on accurate representation of information. Our second group of five questions are of this nature.

For each of Questions 1 through 10, select the paragraph that BEST expresses the ideas contained in the sentences above it. *PRINT THE LETTER OF THE CORRECT ANSWER IN THE SPACE AT THE RIGHT.*

1. I. Listening skills are very important for managers. 1.____
   II. Listening skills are not usually emphasized.
   III. Whenever managers are depicted in books, manuals or the media, they are always talking, never listening.
   IV. We'd like you to read the enclosed handout on listening skills and to try to consciously apply them this week.
   V. We guarantee they will improve the quality of your interactions.

   A. Unfortunately, listening skills are not usually emphasized for managers. Managers are always depicted as talking, never listening. We'd like you to read the enclosed handout on listening skills. Please try to apply these principles this week. If you do, we guarantee they will improve the quality of your interactions.
   B. The enclosed handout on listening skills will be important improving the quality of your interactions. We guarantee it. All you have to do is take sometime this week to read and to consciously try to apply the principles. Listening skills are very important for manages, but they are not usually emphasized. Whenever managers are depicted in books, manuals or the media, they are always talking, never listening.
   C. Listening well is one of the most important skills a manager can have, yet it's not usually given much attention. Think about any representation of managers in books, manuals, or in the media that you may have seen. They're always talking, never listening. We'd like you to read the enclosed handout on listening skills and consciously try to apply them the rest of the week. We guarantee you will see a difference in the quality of your interactions.

D. Effective listening, one very important tool in the effective manager's arsenal, is usually not emphasized enough. The usual depiction of managers in books, manuals or the media is one in which they are always talking, never listening. We'd like you to read the enclosed handout and consciously try to apply the information contained therein throughout the rest of the week. We feel sure that you will see a marked difference in the quality of your interactions.

2. I. Chekhov wrote three dramatic masterpieces which share certain themes and formats: Uncle Vanya, The Cherry Orchard, and The Three Sisters. 2.____

II. They are primarily concerned with the passage of time and how this erodes human aspirations.

III. The plays are haunted by the ghosts of the wasted life.

IV. The characters are concerned with life's lesser problems; however, such as the inability to make decisions, loyalty to the wrong cause, and the inability to be clear.

V. This results in sweet, almost aching, type of a sadness referred to as Chekhovian.

A. Chekhov wrote three dramatic masterpieces: Uncle Vanya, The Cherry Orchard, and The Three Sisters. These masterpieces share certain themes and formats: the passage of time, how time erodes human aspirations, and the ghosts of wasted life. Each masterpiece is characterized by a sweet, almost aching, type of sadness that has become known as Chekhovian. The sweetness of this sadness hinges on the fact that it is not the great tragedies of life which are destroying these characters, but their minor flaws: indecisiveness, misplaced loyalty, unclarity.

B. The Cherry Orchard, Uncle Vanya, and The Three Sisters are three dramatic masterpieces written by Chekhov that use similar formats to explore a common theme. Each is primarily concerned with the way that passing time wears down human aspirations, and each is haunted by the ghosts of the wasted life. The characters are shown struggling futilely with the lesser problems of life: indecisiveness, loyalty to the wrong cause, and the inability to be clear. These struggles create a mood of sweet, almost aching, sadness that has become known as Chekhovian.

C. Chekhov's dramatic masterpieces are, along with The Cherry Orchard, Uncle Vanya, and The Three Sisters. These plays share certain thematic and formal similarities. They are concerned most of all with the passage of time and the way in which time erodes human aspirations. Each play is haunted by the specter of the wasted life. Chekhov's characters are caught, however, by life's lesser snares: indecisiveness, loyalty to the wrong cause, and unclarity. The characteristic mood is a sweet, almost aching type of sadness that has come to be known as Chekhovian.

D. A Chekhovian mood is characterized by sweet, almost aching, sadness. The term comes from three dramatic tragedies by Chekhov which revolve around the sadness of a wasted life. The three masterpieces (Uncle Vanya, The Three Sisters, and The Cherry Orchard) share the same theme and format. The plays are concerned with how the passage of time erodes human aspirations. They are peopled with characters who are struggling with life's lesser problems. These are people who are indecisive, loyal to the wrong causes, or are unable to make themselves clear.

3. I. Movie previews have often helped producers decide which parts of movies they should take out or leave in. 3.____
II. The first 1933 preview of King Kong was very helpful to the producers because many people ran screaming from the theater and would not return when four men first attacked by Kong were eaten by giant spiders.
III. The 1950 premiere of Sunset Boulevard resulted in the filming of an entirely new beginning, and a delay of six months in the film's release.
IV. In the original opening scene, William Holden was in a morgue talking with thirty-six other "corpses" about the ways some of them had died.
V. When he began to tell them of his life with Gloria Swanson, the audience found this hilarious, instead of taking the scene seriously.

A. Movie previews have often helped producers decide what parts of movies they should leave in or take out. For example, the first preview of King Kong in 1933 was very helpful. In one scene, four men were first attacked by Kong and then eaten by giant spiders. Many members of the audience ran screaming from the theater and would not return. The premiere of the 1950 film Sunset Boulevard was also very helpful. In the original opening scene, William Holden was in a morgue with thirty-six other "corpses," discussing the ways some of them had died. When he began to tell them of his life with Gloria Swanson, the audience found this hilarious. They were supposed to take the scene seriously. The result was a delay of six months in the release of the film while a new beginning was added.
B. Movie previews have often helped producers decide whether they should change various parts of a movie. After the 1933 preview of King Kong, a scene in which four men who had been attacked by Kong were eaten by giant spiders was taken out as many people ran screaming from the theater and would not return. The 1950 premiere of Sunset Boulevard also led to some changes. In the original opening scene, William Holden was in a morgue talking with thirty-six other "corpses" about the ways some of them had died. When he began to tell them of his life with Gloria Swanson, the audience found this hilarious, instead of taking the scene seriously.
C. What do Sunset Boulevard and King Kong have in common? Both show the value of using movie previews to test audience reaction. The first 1933 preview of King Kong showed that a scene showing four men being eaten by giant spiders after having been attacked by Kong was too frightening for many people. They ran screaming from the theater and couldn't be coaxed back. The 1950 premiere of Sunset Boulevard was also a scream, but not the kind the producers intended. The movie opens

with William Holden lying in a morgue discussing the ways they had died with thirty-six other "corpses." When he began to tell them of his life with Gloria Swanson, the audience couldn't take him seriously. Their laughter caused a six-month delay while the beginning was rewritten.

D. Producers very often use movie previews to decide if changes are needed. The premiere of Sunset Boulevard in 1950 led to a new beginning and a six-month delay in film release. At the beginning, William Holden and thirty-six other "corpses" discuss the ways some of them died. Rather than taking this seriously, the audience thought it was hilarious when he began to tell them of his life with Gloria Swanson. The first 1933 preview of King Kong was very helpful for its producers because one scene so terrified the audience that many of them ran screaming from the theater and would not return. In this particular scene, four men who had first been attacked by Kong were eaten by giant spiders.

4. I. It is common for supervisors to view employees as "things" to be manipulated. 4.____

II. This approach does not motivate employees, nor does the carrot-and-stick approach because employees often recognize these behaviors and resent them.

III. Supervisors can change these behaviors by using self-inquiry and persistence.

IV. The best managers genuinely respect those they work with, are supportive and helpful, and are interested in working as a team with those they supervise.

V. They disagree with the Golden Rule that says "he or she who has the gold makes the rules."

A. Some managers act as if they think the Golden Rule means "he or she who has the gold makes the rules." They show disrespect to employees by seeing them as "things" to be manipulated. Obviously, this approach does not motivate employees any more than the carrot-and-stick approach motivates them. The employees are smart enough to spot these behaviors and resent them. On the other hand, the managers genuinely respect those they work with, are supportive and helpful, and are interested in working as a team. Self-inquiry and persistence can change even the former type of supervisor into the latter.

B. Many supervisors all into the trap of viewing employees as "things" to be manipulated, or try to motivate them by using a carrot-and-stick approach. These methods do not motivate employees, who often recognize the behaviors and resent them. Supervisors can change these behaviors, however, by using self-inquiry and persistence. The best managers are supportive and helpful, and have genuine respect for those with whom they work. They are interested in working as a team with those they supervise. To them, the Golden Rule is not "he or she who has the gold makes the rules."

C. Some supervisors see employees as "things" to be used or manipulated using a carrot-and-stick technique. These methods don't work. Employees often see through them and resent them. A supervisor who wants to change may do so. The techniques of self-inquiry and persistence can be used to turn him or her into the type of supervisor who doesn't think the Golden Rule is "he or she who has the gold makes the rules." They may become like the best managers who treat those with whom they work with respect and give them help and support. These are the manager who know how to build a team.

D. Unfortunately, many supervisors act as if their employees are objects whose movements they can position at will. This mistaken belief has the same result as another popular motivational technique—the carrot-and-stick approach. Both attitudes can lead to the same result—resentment from those employees who recognize the behaviors for what they are. Supervisors who recognize these behaviors can change through the use of persistence and the use of self-inquiry. It's important to remember that the best managers respect their employees. They readily give necessary help and support and are interested in working as a team with those they supervise. To these managers, the Golden Rule is not "he or she who has the gold makes the rules."

5. I. The first half of the nineteenth century produced a group of pessimistic poets—Byron, De Musset, Heine, Pushkin, and Leopardi. 5.____

II. It also produced a group of pessimistic composers—Schubert, Chopin, Schumann, and even the later Beethoven.

III. Above all, in philosophy, there was the profoundly pessimistic philosopher, Schopenhauer.

IV. The Revolution was dead, the Bourbons were restored, the feudal barons were reclaiming their land, and progress everywhere was being suppressed, as the great age was over.

V. "I thank God," said Goethe, "that I am not young in so thoroughly finished a world."

A. "I thank God," said Goethe, "that I am not young in so thoroughly finished a world." The Revolution was dead, the Bourbons were restored, the feudal barons were reclaiming their land, and progress everywhere was being suppressed. The first half of the nineteenth century produced a group of pessimistic poets: Byron, De Musset, Heine, Pushkin, and Leopardi. It also produced pessimistic composers: Schubert, Chopin, Schumann. Although Beethoven came later, he fits into this group, too. Finally and above all, it also produced a profoundly pessimistic philosopher, Schopenhauer. The great age was over.

B. The first half of the nineteenth century produced a group of pessimistic poets: Byron, De Musset, Heine, Pushkin, and Leopardi. It produced a group of pessimistic composers: Schubert, Chopin, Schumann, and even the later Beethoven. Above all, it produced a profoundly pessimistic philosopher, Schopenhauer. For each of these men, the great age was over. The Revolution was dead, and the Bourbons were restored. The feudal barons were reclaiming their land, and progress everywhere was being suppressed.

C. The great age was over. The Revolution was dead—the Bourbons were restored, and the feudal barons were reclaiming their land. Progress everywhere was being suppressed. Out of this climate came a profound pessimism. Poets, like Byron, De Musset, Heine, Pushkin, and Leopardi; composers, like Schubert, Chopin, Schumann, and even the later Beethoven; and above all, a profoundly pessimistic philosopher, Schopenauer. This pessimism which arose in the first half of the nineteenth century is illustrated by these words of Goethe, "I thank God that I am not young in so thoroughly finished a world."

D. The first half of the nineteenth century produced a group of pessimistic poets, Byron, De Musset, Heine, Pushkin, and Leopardi—and a group of pessimistic composers, Schubert, Chopin, Schumann, and the later Beethoven. Above it all, it produced a profoundly pessimistic philosopher, Schopenhauer. The great age was over. The Revolution was dead, the Bourbons were restored, the feudal barons were reclaiming their land, and progress everywhere was being suppressed. "I thank God," said Goethe, "that I am not young in so thoroughly finished a world."

6. I. A new manager sometimes may feel insecure about his or her competence in the new position. 6.____

II. The new manager may then exhibit defensive or arrogant behavior towards those one supervises, or the new manager may direct overly flattering behavior toward one's new supervisor.

A. Sometimes, a new manager may feel insecure about his or her ability to perform well in this new position. The insecurity may lead him or her to treat others differently. He or she may display arrogant or defensive behavior towards those he or she supervises, or be overly flattering to his or her new supervisor.

B. A new manager may sometimes feel insecure about his or her ability to perform well in the new position. He or she may then become arrogant, defensive, or overly flattering towards those he or she works with.

C. There are times when a new manager may be insecure about how well he or she can perform in the new job. The new manager may also behave defensive or act in an arrogant way towards those he or she supervises, or overly flatter his or her boss.

D. Sometimes a new manager may feel insecure about his or her ability to perform well in the new position. He or she may then display arrogant or defensive behavior towards those they supervise, or become overly flattering towards their supervisors.

7. I. It is possible to eliminate unwanted behavior by bringing it under stimulus control—tying the behavior to a cue, and then never, or rarely, giving the cue. 7.____

II. One trainer successfully used this method to keep an energetic young porpoise from coming out of her tank whenever she felt like it, which was potentially dangerous.

III. Her trainer taught her to do it for a reward, in response to a hand signal, and then rarely gave the signal.

A. Unwanted behavior can be eliminated by tying the behavior to a cue, and then never, or rarely, giving the cue. This is called stimulus control. One trainer was able to use this method to keep an energetic young porpoise from coming out of her tank by teaching her to come out for a reward in response to a hand signal, and then rarely giving the signal.
B. Stimulus control can be used to eliminate unwanted behavior. In this method, behavior is tied to a cue, and then the cue is rarely, if ever, given. One trainer was able to successfully use stimulus control to keep an energetic young porpoise from coming out of her tank whenever she felt like it—a potentially dangerous practice. She taught the porpoise to come out for a reward when she gave a hand signal, and then rarely gave the signal.
C. It is possible to eliminate behavior that is undesirable by bringing it under stimulus control by tying behavior to a signal, and then rarely giving the signal. One trainer successfully used this method to keep an energetic porpoise from coming out of her tank, a potentially dangerous situation. Her trainer taught the porpoise to do it for a reward, in response to a hand signal, and then would rarely give the signal.
D. By using stimulus control, it is possible to eliminate unwanted behavior by tying the behavior to a cue, and then rarely or never give the cue. One trainer was able to use this method to successfully stop a young porpoise from coming out of her tank whenever she felt like it. To curb this potentially dangerous practice, the porpoise was taught by the trainer to come out of the tank for a reward, in response to a hand signal, and then rarely given the signal.

8. I. There is a great deal of concern over the safety of commercial trucks, caused by their greatly increased role in serious accidents since federal deregulation in 1981. 8.____
II. Recently, 60 percent of trucks in New York and Connecticut and 70 percent of trucks in Maryland randomly stopped by state troopers failed safety inspections.
III. Sixteen states in the United States require no training at all for truck drivers.

A. Since federal deregulation in 1981, there has been a great deal of concern over the safety of commercial trucks, and their greatly increased role in serious accidents. Recently, 60 percent of trucks in New York and Connecticut, and 70 percent of trucks in Maryland failed safety inspections. Sixteen states in the United States require no training at all for truck drivers.
B. There is a great deal of concern over the safety of commercial trucks since federal deregulation in 1981. Their role in serious accidents has greatly increased. Recently, 60 percent of trucks randomly stopped in Connecticut and New York and 70 percent in Maryland failed safety inspections conducted by state troopers. Sixteen states in the United States provide no training at all for truck drivers.
C. Commercial trucks have a greatly increased role in serious accidents since federal deregulation in 1981. This has led to a great deal of concern.

Recently, 70 percent of trucks in Maryland and 60 percent of trucks in New York and Connecticut failed inspection of those that were randomly stopped by state troopers. Sixteen states in the United States require no training for all truck drivers.

D. Since federal deregulation in 1981, the role that commercial trucks have played in serious accidents has greatly increased, and this has led to a great deal of concern. Recently, 60 percent of trucks in New York and Connecticut, and 70 percent of trucks in Maryland randomly stopped by state troopers failed safety inspections. Sixteen states in the U.S. don't require any training for truck drivers.

9. I. No matter how much some people have, they still feel unsatisfied and want more, or want to keep what they have forever. 9.____

II. One recent television documentary showed several people flying from New York to Paris for a one-day shopping spree to buy platinum earrings, because they were bored.

III. In Brazil, some people were ordering coffins that cost a minimum of $45,000 and are equipping them with deluxe stereos, televisions, and other graveyard necessities.

A. Some people, despite having a great deal, still feel unsatisfied and want more, or think they can keep what they have forever. One recent documentary on television showed several people enroute from Paris to New York for a one day shopping spree to buy platinum earrings, because they were bored. Some people in Brazil are even ordering coffins equipped with such graveyard necessities as deluxe stereos and televisions. The price of the coffins start at $45,000.

B. No matter how much some people have, they may feel unsatisfied. This leads them to want more, or to want to keep what they have forever. Recently, a television documentary depicting several people flying from New York to Paris for a one day shopping spree to buy platinum earrings. They were bored. Some people in Brazil are ordering coffins that cost at least $45,000 and come equipped with deluxe televisions, stereos and other necessary graveyard items.

C. Some people will be dissatisfied no matter how much they have. They may want more, or they may want to keep what they have forever. One recent television documentary showed several people, motivated by boredom, jetting from New York to Paris for a one-day shopping spree to buy platinum earrings. In Brazil, some people are ordering coffins equipped with deluxe stereos, televisions and other graveyard necessities. The minimum price for these coffins—$45,000.

D. Some people are never satisfied. No matter how much they have they still want more, or think they can keep what they have forever. One television documentary recently showed several people flying from New York to Paris for the day to buy platinum earrings because they were bored. In Brazil, some people are ordering coffins that cost $45,000 and are equipped with deluxe stereos, televisions and other graveyard necessities.

10. I. A television signal or video signal has three parts. 10.____
II. Its parts are the black-and-white portion, the color portion, and the synchronizing (sync) pulses, which keep the picture stable.
III. Each video source, whether it's a camera or a video-cassette recorder contains its own generator of these synchronizing pulses to accompany the picture that it's sending in order to keep it steady and straight.
IV. In order to produce a clean recording, a video-cassette recorder must "lock-up" to the sync pulses that are part of the video it is trying to record, and this effort may be very noticeable if the device does not have gunlock.

A. There are three parts to a television or video signal: the black-and-white part, the color part, and the synchronizing (sync) pulses, which keep the picture stable. Whether it's a video-cassette recorder or a camera, each video source contains its own pulse that synchronizes and generates the picture it's sending in order to keep it straight and steady. A video-cassette recorder must "lock up" to the sync pulses that are part of the video it's trying to record. If the device doesn't have gunlock, this effort must be very noticeable.
B. A video signal or television is comprised of three parts: the black-and-white portion, the color portion, and the sync (synchronizing) pulses, which keep the picture stable. Whether it's a camera or a video-cassette recorder, each video source contains its own generator of these synchronizing pulses. These accompany the picture that it's sending in order to keep it straight and steady. A video-cassette recorder must "lock up" to the sync pulses that are part of the video it is trying to record in order to produce a clean recording. This effort may be very noticeable if the device does not have gunlock.
C. There are three parts to a television or video signal: the color portion, the black-and-white portion, and the sync (synchronizing pulses). These keep the picture stable. Each video source, whether it's a video-cassette recorder or a camera, generates these synchronizing pulses accompanying the picture it's sending in order to keep it straight and steady. If a clean recording is to be produced, a video-cassette recorder must store the sync pulses that are part of the video it is trying to record. This effort may not be noticeable if the device does not have gunlock.
D. A television signal or video signal has three parts: the black-and-white portion, the color portion, and the synchronizing (sync) pulses. It's the sync pulses which keep the picture stable, which accompany it and keep it steady and straight. Whether it's a camera or a video-cassette recorder, each video source contains its own generator of these synchronizing pulses. To produce a clean recording, a video-cassette recorder must "lock up" to the sync pulses that are part of the video it is trying to record. If the device does not have gunlock, this effort may be very noticeable.

KEY (CORRECT ANSWERS)

1.	C	6.	A
2.	B	7.	B
3.	A	8.	D
4.	B	9.	C
5.	D	10.	D

PHILOSOPHY, PRINCIPLES, PRACTICES, AND TECHNICS
OF
SUPERVISION, ADMINISTRATION, MANAGEMENT, AND ORGANIZATION

TABLE OF CONTENTS

	Page
MEANING OF SUPERVISION	1
THE OLD AND THE NEW SUPERVISION	1
THE EIGHT (8) BASIC PRINCIPLES OF THE NEW SUPERVISION	1
I. Principle of Responsibility	1
II. Principle of Authority	2
III. Principle of Self-Growth	2
IV. Principle of Individual Worth	2
V. Principle of Creative Leadership	2
VI. Principle of Success and Failure	2
VII. Principle of Science	3
VIII. Principle of Cooperation	3
WHAT IS ADMINISTRATION?	3
I. Practices Commonly Classed as "Supervisory"	3
II. Practices Commonly Classed as "Administrative"	3
III. Practices Commonly Classed as Both "Supervisory" and "Administrative"	4
RESPONSIBILITIES OF THE SUPERVISOR	4
COMPETENCIES OF THE SUPERVISOR	4
THE PROFESSIONAL SUPERVISOR-EMPLOYEE RELATIONSHIP	4
MINI-TEXT IN SUPERVISION, ADMINISTRATION, MANAGEMENT, AND ORGANIZATION	5
I. Brief Highlights	5
A. Levels of Management	6
B. What the Supervisor Must Learn	6
C. A Definition of Supervision	6
D. Elements of the Team Concept	6
E. Principles of Organization	6
F. The Four Important Parts of Every Job	7
G. Principles of Delegation	7
H. Principles of Effective Communications	7
I. Principles of Work Improvement	7
J. Areas of Job Improvement	7
K. Seven Key Points in Making Improvements	8

L. Corrective Techniques for Job Improvement 8
M. A Planning Checklist 8
N. Five Characteristics of Good Directions 9
O. Types of Directions 9
P. Controls 9
Q. Orienting the New Employee 9
R. Checklist for Orienting New Employees 9
S. Principles of Learning 10
T. Causes of Poor Performance 10
U. Four Major Steps in On-the-Job Instructions 10
V. Employees Want Five Things 10
W. Some Don'ts in Regard to Praise 11
X. How to Gain Your Workers' Confidence 11
Y. Sources of Employee Problems 11
Z. The Supervisor's Key to Discipline 11
AA. Five Important Processes of Management 12
BB. When the Supervisor Fails to Plan 12
CC. Fourteen General Principles of Management 12
DD. Change 12

II. Brief Topical Summaries 13
A. Who/What is the Supervisor? 13
B. The Sociology of Work 13
C. Principles and Practices of Supervision 14
D. Dynamic Leadership 14
E. Processes for Solving Problems 15
F. Training for Results 15
G. Health, Safety, and Accident Prevention 16
H. Equal Employment Opportunity 16
I. Improving Communications 16
J. Self-Development 17
K. Teaching and Training 17
1. The Teaching Process 17
a. Preparation 17
b. Presentation 18
c. Summary 18
d. Application 18
e. Evaluation 18
2. Teaching Methods 18
a. Lecture 18
b. Discussion 18
c. Demonstration 19
d. Performance 19
e. Which Method to Use 19

PHILOSOPHY, PRINCIPLES, PRACTICES, AND TECHNICS
OF
SUPERVISION, ADMINISTRATION, MANAGEMENT, AND ORGANIZATION

MEANING OF SUPERVISION

The extension of the democratic philosophy has been accompanied by an extension in the scope of supervision. Modern leaders and supervisors no longer think of supervision in the narrow sense of being confined chiefly to visiting employees, supplying materials, or rating the staff. They regard supervision as being intimately related to all the concerned agencies of society, they speak of the supervisor's function in terms of "growth," rather than the "improvement" of employees.

This modern concept of supervision may be defined as follows: Supervision is leadership and the development of leadership within groups which are cooperatively engaged in inspection, research, training, guidance, and evaluation.

THE OLD AND THE NEW SUPERVISION

<u>TRADITIONAL</u>
1. Inspection
2. Focused on the employee
3. Visitation
4. Random and haphazard
5. Imposed and authoritarian
6. One person usually

<u>MODERN</u>
1. Study and analysis
2. Focused on aims, materials, methods, supervisors, employees, environment
3. Demonstrations, intervisitation, workshops, directed reading, bulletins, etc.
4. Definitely organized and planned (scientific)
5. Cooperative and democratic
6. Many persons involved (creative)

THE EIGHT (8) BASIC PRINCIPLES OF THE NEW SUPERVISION

I. Principle of Responsibility
Authority to act and responsibility for acting must be joined.
A. If you give responsibility, give authority.
B. Define employee duties clearly.
C. Protect employees from criticism by others.
D. Recognize the rights as well as obligations of employees.
E. Achieve the aims of a democratic society insofar as it is possible within the area of your work.
F. Establish a situation favorable to training and learning.
G. Accept ultimate responsibility for everything done in your section, unit, office, division, department.
H. Good administration and good supervision are inseparable.

II. Principle of Authority
The success of the supervisor is measured by the extent to which the power of authority is not used.
A. Exercise simplicity and informality in supervision
B. Use the simplest machinery of supervision
C. If it is good for the organization as a whole, it is probably justified.
D. Seldom be arbitrary or authoritative.
E. Do not base your work on the power of position or of personality.
F. Permit and encourage the free expression of opinions.

III. Principle of Self-Growth
The success of the supervisor is measured by the extent to which, and the speed with which, he is no longer needed.
A. Base criticism on principles, not on specifics.
B. Point out higher activities to employees.
C. Train for self-thinking by employees to meet new situations.
D. Stimulate initiative, self-reliance, and individual responsibility
E. Concentrate on stimulating the growth of employees rather than on removing defects.

IV. Principle of Individual Worth
Respect for the individual is a paramount consideration in supervision.
A. Be human and sympathetic in dealing with employees.
B. Don't nag about things to be done.
C. Recognize the individual differences among employees and seek opportunities to permit best expression of each personality.

V. Principle of Creative Leadership
The best supervision is that which is not apparent to the employee.
A. Stimulate, don't drive employees to creative action.
B. Emphasize doing good things.
C. Encourage employees to do what they do best.
D. Do not be too greatly concerned with details of subject or method.
E. Do not be concerned exclusively with immediate problems and activities.
F. Reveal higher activities and make them both desired and maximally possible.
G. Determine procedures in the light of each situation but see that these are derived from a sound basic philosophy.
H. Aid, inspire, and lead so as to liberate the creative spirit latent in all good employees.

VI. Principle of Success and Failure
There are no unsuccessful employees, only unsuccessful supervisors who have failed to give proper leadership.
A. Adapt suggestions to the capacities, attitudes, and prejudices of employees.
B. Be gradual, be progressive, be persistent.
C. Help the employee find the general principle; have the employee apply his own problem to the general principle.
D. Give adequate appreciation for good work and honest effort.
E. Anticipate employee difficulties and help to prevent them.
F. Encourage employees to do the desirable things they will do anyway.
G. Judge your supervision by the results it secures.

VII. Principle of Science
Successful supervision is scientific, objective, and experimental. It is based on facts, not on prejudices.
A. Be cumulative in results.
B. Never divorce your suggestions from the goals of training.
C. Don't be impatient of results.
D. Keep all matters on a professional, not a personal, level.
E. Do not be concerned exclusively with immediate problems and activities.
F. Use objective means of determining achievement and rating where possible.

VIII. Principle of Cooperation
Supervision is a cooperative enterprise between supervisor and employee.
A. Begin with conditions as they are.
B. Ask opinions of all involved when formulating policies.
C. Organization is as good as its weakest link.
D. Let employees help to determine policies and department programs.
E. Be approachable and accessible—physically and mentally.
F. Develop pleasant social relationships.

WHAT IS ADMINISTRATION

Administration is concerned with providing the environment, the material facilities, and the operational procedures that will promote the maximum growth and development of supervisors and employees. (Organization is an aspect and a concomitant of administration.)

There is no sharp line of demarcation between supervision and administration; these functions are intimately interrelated and, often, overlapping. They are complementary activities.

I. Practices Commonly Classed as "Supervisory"
A. Conducting employees' conferences
B. Visiting sections, units, offices, divisions, departments
C. Arranging for demonstrations
D. Examining plans
E. Suggesting professional reading
F. Interpreting bulletins
G. Recommending in-service training courses
H. Encouraging experimentation
I. Appraising employee morale
J. Providing for intervisitation

II. Practices Commonly Classified as "Administrative"
A. Management of the office
B. Arrangement of schedules for extra duties
C. Assignment of rooms or areas
D. Distribution of supplies
E. Keeping records and reports
F. Care of audio-visual materials
G. Keeping inventory records
H. Checking record cards and books

I. Programming special activities
J. Checking on the attendance and punctuality of employees

III. Practices Commonly Classified as Both "Supervisory" and "Administrative"
   A. Program construction
   B. Testing or evaluating outcomes
   C. Personnel accounting
   D. Ordering instructional materials

RESPONSIBILITIES OF THE SUPERVISOR

A person employed in a supervisory capacity must constantly be able to improve his own efficiency and ability. He represent the employer to the employees and only continuous self-examination can make him a capable supervisor.

Leadership and training are the supervisor's responsibility. An efficient working unit is one in which the employees work with the supervisor. It is his job to bring out the best in his employees. He must always be relaxed, courteous, and calm in his association with his employees. Their feelings are important, and a harsh attitude does not develop the most efficient employees.

COMPETENCES OF THE SUPERVISOR

I. Complete knowledge of the duties and responsibilities of his position.
II. To be able to organize a job, plan ahead, and carry through.
III. To have self-confidence and initiative.
IV. To be able to handle the unexpected situation and make quick decisions.
V. To be able to properly train subordinates in the positions they are best suited for.
VI. To be able to keep good human relations among his subordinates.
VII. To be able to keep good human relations between his subordinates and himself and to earn their respect and trust.

THE PROFESSIONAL SUPERVISOR-EMPLOYEE RELATIONSHIP

There are two kinds of efficiency: one kind is only apparent and is produced in organizations through the exercise of mere discipline; this is but a simulation of the second, or true, efficiency which springs from spontaneous cooperation. If you are a manager, no matter how great or small your responsibility, it is your job, in the final analysis, to create and develop this involuntary cooperation among the people whom you supervise. For, no matter how powerful a combination of money, machines, and materials a company may have, this is a dead and sterile thing without a team of willing, thinking, and articulate people to guide it.

The following 21 points are presented as indicative of the exemplary basic relationship that should exist between supervisor and employee:

1. Each person wants to be liked and respected by his fellow employee and wants to be treated with consideration and respect by his superior.
2. The most competent employee will make an error. However, in a unit where good relations exist between the supervisor and his employees, tenseness and fear do not exist. Thus, errors are not hidden or covered up, and the efficiency of a unit is not impaired.

3. Subordinates resent rules, regulations, or orders that are unreasonable or unexplained.
4. Subordinates are quick to resent unfairness, harshness, injustices, and favoritism.
5. An employee will accept responsibility if he knows that he will be complimented for a job well done, and not too harshly chastised for failure; that his supervisor will check the cause of the failure, and, if it was the supervisor's fault, he will assume the blame therefore. If it was the employee's fault, his supervisor will explain the correct method or means of handling the responsibility.
6. An employee wants to receive credit for a suggestion he has made, that is used. If a suggestion cannot be used, the employee is entitled to an explanation. The supervisor should not say "no" and close the subject.
7. Fear and worry slow up a worker's ability. Poor working environment can impair his physical and mental health. A good supervisor avoids forceful methods, threats, and arguments to get a job done.
8. A forceful supervisor is able to train his employees individually and as a team, and is able to motivate them in the proper channels.
9. A mature supervisor is able to properly evaluate his subordinates and to keep them happy and satisfied.
10. A sensitive supervisor will never patronize his subordinates.
11. A worthy supervisor will respect his employees' confidences.
12. Definite and clear-cut responsibilities should be assigned to each executive.
13. Responsibility should always be coupled with corresponding authority.
14. No change should be made in the scope or responsibilities of a position without a definite understanding to that effect on the part of all persons concerned.
15. No executive or employee, occupying a single position in the organization, should be subject to definite orders from more than one source.
16. Orders should never be given to subordinates over the head of a responsible executive. Rather than do this, the officer in question should be supplanted.
17. Criticisms of subordinates should, whoever possible, be made privately, and in no case should a subordinate be criticized in the presence of executives or employees of equal or lower rank.
18. No dispute or difference between executives or employees as to authority or responsibilities should be considered too trivial for prompt and careful adjudication.
19. Promotions, wage changes, and disciplinary action should always be approved by the executive immediately superior to the one directly responsible.
20. No executive or employee should ever be required, or expected, to be at the same time an assistant to, and critic of, another.
21. Any executive whose work is subject to regular inspection should, wherever practicable, be given the assistance and facilities necessary to enable him to maintain an independent check of the quality of his work.

MINI-TEXT IN SUPERVISION, ADMINISTRATION, MANAGEMENT, AND ORGANIZATION

I. Brief Highlights

Listed concisely and sequentially are major headings and important data in the field for quick recall and review.

A. Levels of Management

Any organization of some size has several levels of management. In terms of a ladder, the levels are:

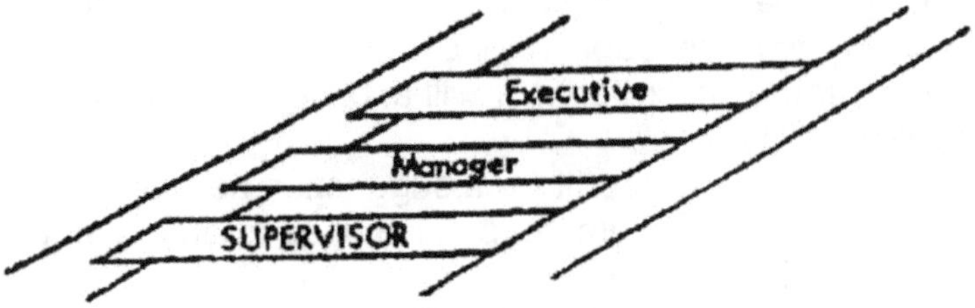

The first level is very important because it is the beginning point of management leadership.

B. What the Supervisor Must Learn

A supervisor must learn to:

1. Deal with people and their differences
2. Get the job done through people
3. Recognize the problems when they exist
4. Overcome obstacles to good performance
5. Evaluate the performance of people
6. Check his own performance in terms of accomplishment

C. A Definition of Supervisor

The term supervisor means any individual having authority, in the interests of the employer, to hire, transfer, suspend, lay-off, recall, promote, discharge, assign, reward, or discipline other employees or responsibility to direct them, or to adjust their grievances, or effectively to recommend such action, if, in connection with the foregoing, exercise of such authority is not of a merely routine or clerical nature but requires the use of independent judgment.

D. Elements of the Team Concept

What is involved in teamwork? The component parts are:

1. Members
2. A leader
3. Goals
4. Plans
5. Cooperation
6. Spirit

E. Principles of Organization

1. A team member must know what his job is.
2. Be sure that the nature and scope of a job are understood.
3. Authority and responsibility should be carefully spelled out.
4. A supervisor should be permitted to make the maximum number of decisions affecting his employees.
5. Employees should report to only one supervisor.
6. A supervisor should direct only as many employees as he can handle effectively.
7. An organization plan should be flexible.

8. Inspection and performance of work should be separate.
9. Organizational problems should receive immediate attention.
10. Assign work in line with ability and experience.

F. The Four Important Parts of Every Job

1. Inherent in every job is the *accountability* for results.
2. A second set of factors in every job is *responsibilities.*
3. Along with duties and responsibilities one must have the *authority* to act within certain limits without obtaining permission to proceed.
4. No job exists in a vacuum. The supervisor is surrounded by key *relationships.*

G. Principles of Delegation

Where work is delegated for the first time, the supervisor should think in terms of these questions:

1. Who is best qualified to do this?
2. Can an employee improve his abilities by doing this?
3. How long should an employee spend on this?
4. Are there any special problems for which he will need guidance?
5. How broad a delegation can I make?

H. Principles of Effective Communications

1. Determine the media.
2. To whom directed?
3. Identification and source authority.
4. Is communication understood?

I. Principles of Work Improvement

1. Most people usually do only the work which is assigned to them.
2. Workers are likely to fit assigned work into the time available to perform it.
3. A good workload usually stimulates output.
4. People usually do their best work when they know that results will be reviewed or inspected.
5. Employees usually feel that someone else is responsible for conditions of work, workplace layout, job methods, type of tools/equipment, and other such factors.
6. Employees are usually defensive about their job security.
7. Employees have natural resistance to change.
8. Employees can support or destroy a supervisor.
9. A supervisor usually earns the respect of his people through his personal example of diligence and efficiency.

J. Areas of Job Improvement

The areas of job improvement are quite numerous, but the most common ones which a supervisor can identify and utilize are:

1. Departmental layout
2. Flow of work
3. Workplace layout
4. Utilization of manpower
5. Work methods
6. Materials handling

7. Utilization
8. Motion economy

K. Seven Key Points in Making Improvements
1. Select the job to be improved
2. Study how it is being done now
3. Question the present method
4. Determine actions to be taken
5. Chart proposed method
6. Get approval and apply
7. Solicit worker participation

I. Corrective Techniques of Job Improvement

Specific Problems
1. Size of workload
2. Inability to meet schedules
3. Strain and fatigue
4. Improper use of men and skills
5. Waste, poor quality, unsafe conditions
6. Bottleneck conditions that hinder output
7. Poor utilization of equipment and machine
8. Efficiency and productivity of labor

General Improvement
1. Departmental layout
2. Flow of work
3. Work plan layout
4. Utilization of manpower
5. Work methods
6. Materials handling
7. Utilization of equipment
8. Motion economy

Corrective Techniques
1. Study with scale model
2. Flow chart study
3. Motion analysis
4. Comparison of units produced to standard allowance
5. Methods analysis
6. Flow chart and equipment study
7. Down time vs. running time
8. Motion analysis

M. A Planning Checklist
1. Objectives
2. Controls
3. Delegations
4. Communications
5. Resources
6. Manpower

7. Equipment
8. Supplies and materials
9. Utilization of time
10. Safety
11. Money
12. Work
13. Timing of improvements

N. Five Characteristics of Good Directions

In order to get results, directions must be:

1. Possible of accomplishment
2. Agreeable with worker interests
3. Related to mission
4. Planned and complete
5. Unmistakably clear

O. Types of Directions

1. Demands or direct orders
2. Requests
3. Suggestion or implication
4. volunteering

P. Controls

A typical listing of the overall areas in which the supervisor should establish controls might be:

1. Manpower
2. Materials
3. Quality of work
4. Quantity of work
5. Time
6. Space
7. Money
8. Methods

Q. Orienting the New Employee

1. Prepare for him
2. Welcome the new employee
3. Orientation for the job
4. Follow-up

R. Checklist for Orienting New Employees

	Yes	No
1. Do you appreciate the feelings of new employees when they first report for work?	___	___
2. Are you aware of the fact that the new employee must make a big adjustment to his job?	___	___
3. Have you given him good reasons for liking the job and the organization?	___	___
4. Have you prepared for his first day on the job?	___	___
5. Did you welcome him cordially and make him feel needed?	___	___

		Yes	No
6.	Did you establish rapport with him so that he feels free to talk and discuss matters with you?	___	___
7.	Did you explain his job to him and his relationship to you?	___	___
8.	Does he know that his work will be evaluated periodically on a basis that is fair and objective?	___	___
9.	Did you introduce him to his fellow workers in such a way that they are likely to accept him?	___	___
10.	Does he know what employee benefits he will receive?	___	___
11.	Does he understand the importance of being on the job and what to do if he must leave his duty station?	___	___
12.	Has he been impressed with the importance of accident prevention and safe practice?	___	___
13.	Does he generally know his way around the department?	___	___
14.	Is he under the guidance of a sponsor who will teach the right way of doing things?	___	___
15.	Do you plan to follow-up so that he will continue to adjust successfully to his job?	___	___

S. Principles of Learning
1. Motivation
2. Demonstration or explanation
3. Practice

T. Causes of Poor Performance
1. Improper training for job
2. Wrong tools
3. Inadequate directions
4. Lack of supervisory follow-up
5. Poor communications
6. Lack of standards of performance
7. Wrong work habits
8. Low morale
9. Other

U. Four Major Steps in On-The-Job Instruction
1. Prepare the worker
2. Present the operation
3. Tryout performance
4. Follow-up

V. Employees Want Five Things
1. Security
2. Opportunity
3. Recognition
4. Inclusion
5. Expression

W. Some Don'ts in Regard to Praise
1. Don't praise a person for something he hasn't done.
2. Don't praise a person unless you can be sincere.
3. Don't be sparing in praise just because your superior withholds it from you.
4. Don't let too much time elapse between good performance and recognition of it

X. How to Gain Your Workers' Confidence

Methods of developing confidence include such things as:
1. Knowing the interests, habits, hobbies of employees
2. Admitting your own inadequacies
3. Sharing and telling of confidence in others
4. Supporting people when they are in trouble
5. Delegating matters that can be well handled
6. Being frank and straightforward about problems and working conditions
7. Encouraging others to bring their problems to you
8. Taking action on problems which impede worker progress

Y. Sources of Employee Problems

On-the-job causes might be such things as:
1. A feeling that favoritism is exercised in assignments
2. Assignment of overtime
3. An undue amount of supervision
4. Changing methods or systems
5. Stealing of ideas or trade secrets
6. Lack of interest in job
7. Threat of reduction in force
8. Ignorance or lack of communications
9. Poor equipment
10. Lack of knowing how supervisor feels toward employee
11. Shift assignments

Off-the-job problems might have to do with:
1. Health
2. Finances
3. Housing
4. Family

Z. The Supervisor's Key to Discipline

There are several key points about discipline which the supervisor should keep in mind:
1. Job discipline is one of the disciplines of life and is directed by the supervisor.
2. It is more important to correct an employee fault than to fix blame for it.
3. Employee performance is affected by problems both on the job and off.
4. Sudden or abrupt changes in behavior can be indications of important employee problems.
5. Problems should be dealt with as soon as possible after they are identified.
6. The attitude of the supervisor may have more to do with solving problems than the techniques of problem solving.
7. Correction of employee behavior should be resorted to only after the supervisor is sure that training or counseling will not be helpful.

8. Be sure to document your disciplinary actions.
9. Make sure that you are disciplining on the basis of facts rather than personal feelings.
10. Take each disciplinary step in order, being careful not to make snap judgments, or decisions based on impatience.

AA. Five Important Processes of Management
1. Planning
2. Organizing
3. Scheduling
4. Controlling
5. Motivating

BB. When the Supervisor Fails to Plan
1. Supervisor creates impression of not knowing his job
2. May lead to excessive overtime
3. Job runs itself—supervisor lacks control
4. Deadlines and appointments missed
5. Parts of the work go undone
6. Work interrupted by emergencies
7. Sets a bad example
8. Uneven workload creates peaks and valleys
9. Too much time on minor details at expense of more important tasks

CC. Fourteen General Principles of Management
1. Division of work
2. Authority and responsibility
3. Discipline
4. Unity of command
5. Unity of direction
6. Subordination of individual interest to general interest
7. Remuneration of personnel
8. Centralization
9. Scalar chain
10. Order
11. Equity
12. Stability of tenure of personnel
13. Initiative
14. Esprit de corps

DD. Change

Bringing about change is perhaps attempted more often, and yet less well understood, than anything else the supervisor does. How do people generally react to change? (People tend to resist change that is imposed upon them by other individuals or circumstances.

Change is characteristic of every situation. It is a part of every real endeavor where the efforts of people are concerned.

1. Why do people resist change?
   People may resist change because of:
   a. Fear of the unknown
   b. Implied criticism
   c. Unpleasant experiences in the past
   d. Fear of loss of status
   e. Threat to the ego
   f. Fear of loss of economic stability

2. How can we best overcome the resistance to change?
   In initiating change, take these steps:
   a. Get ready to sell
   b. Identify sources of help
   c. Anticipate objections
   d. Sell benefits
   e. Listen in depth
   f. Follow up

II. Brief Topical Summaries

A. Who/What is the Supervisor?
   1. The supervisor is often called the "highest level employee and the lowest level manager."
   2. A supervisor is a member of both management and the work group. He acts as a bridge between the two.
   3. Most problems in supervision are in the area of human relations, or people problems.
   4. Employees expect: Respect, opportunity to learn and to advance, and a sense of belonging, and so forth.
   5. Supervisors are responsible for directing people and organizing work. Planning is of paramount importance.
   6. A position description is a set of duties and responsibilities inherent to a given position.
   7. It is important to keep the position description up-to-date and to provide each employee with his own copy.

B. The Sociology of Work
   1. People are alike in many ways; however, each individual is unique.
   2. The supervisor is challenged in getting to know employee differences. Acquiring skills in evaluating individuals is an asset.
   3. Maintaining meaningful working relationships in the organization is of great importance.
   4. The supervisor has an obligation to help individuals to develop to their fullest potential.
   5. Job rotation on a planned basis helps to build versatility and to maintain interest and enthusiasm in work groups.
   6. Cross training (job rotation) provides backup skills.

7. The supervisor can help reduce tension by maintaining a sense of humor, providing guidance to employees, and by making reasonable and timely decisions. Employees respond favorably to working under reasonably predictable circumstances.
8. Change is characteristic of all managerial behavior. The supervisor must adjust to changes in procedures, new methods, technological changes, and to a number of new and sometimes challenging situations.
9. To overcome the natural tendency for people to resist change, the supervisor should become more skillful in initiating change.

C. Principles and Practices of Supervision

1. Employees should be required to answer to only one superior.
2. A supervisor can effectively direct only a limited number of employees, depending upon the complexity, variety, and proximity of the jobs involved.
3. The organizational chart presents the organization in graphic form. It reflects lines of authority and responsibility as well as interrelationships of units within the organization.
4. Distribution of work can be improved through an analysis using the "Work Distribution Chart."
5. The "Work Distribution Chart" reflects the division of work within a unit in understandable form.
6. When related tasks are given to an employee, he has a better chance of increasing his skills through training.
7. The individual who is given the responsibility for tasks must also be given the appropriate authority to insure adequate results.
8. The supervisor should delegate repetitive, routine work. Preparation of recurring reports, maintaining leave and attendance records are some examples.
9. Good discipline is essential to good task performance. Discipline is reflected in the actions of employees on the job in the absence of supervision.
10. Disciplinary action may have to be taken when the positive aspects of discipline have failed. Reprimand, warning, and suspension are examples of disciplinary action.
11. If a situation calls for a reprimand, be sure it is deserved and remember it is to be done in private.

D. Dynamic Leadership

1. A style is a personal method or manner of exerting influence.
2. Authoritarian leaders often see themselves as the source of power and authority.
3. The democratic leader often perceives the group as the source of authority and power.
4. Supervisors tend to do better when using the pattern of leadership that is most natural for them.
5. Social scientists suggest that the effective supervisor use the leadership style that best fits the problem or circumstances involved.
6. All four styles—telling, selling, consulting, joining—have their place. Using one does not preclude using the other at another time.

7. The theory X point of view assumes that the average person dislikes work, will avoid it whenever possible, and must be coerced to achieve organizational objectives.
8. The theory Y point of view assumes that the average person considers work to be a natural as play, and, when the individual is committed, he requires little supervision or direction to accomplish desired objectives.
9. The leader's basic assumptions concerning human behavior and human nature affect his actions, decisions, and other managerial practices.
10. Dissatisfaction among employees is often present, but difficult to isolate. The supervisor should seek to weaken dissatisfaction by keeping promises, being sincere and considerate, keeping employees informed, and so forth.
11. Constructive suggestions should be encouraged during the natural progress of the work.

E. Processes for Solving Problems

1. People find their daily tasks more meaningful and satisfying when they can improve them.
2. The causes of problems, or the key factors, are often hidden in the background. Ability to solve problems often involves the ability to isolate them from their backgrounds. There is some substance to the cliché that some persons "can't see the forest for the trees."
3. New procedures are often developed from old ones. Problems should be broken down into manageable parts. New ideas can be adapted from old one.
4. People think differently in problem-solving situations. Using a logical, patterned approach is often useful. One approach found to be useful includes these steps:
   a. Define the problem
   b. Establish objectives
   c. Get the facts
   d. Weigh and decide
   e. Take action
   f. Evaluate action

F. Training for Results

1. Participants respond best when they feel training is important to them.
2. The supervisor has responsibility for the training and development of those who report to him.
3. When training is delegated to others, great care must be exercised to insure the trainer has knowledge, aptitude, and interest for his work as a trainer.
4. Training (learning) of some type goes on continually. The most successful supervisor makes certain the learning contributes in a productive manner to operational goals.
5. New employees are particularly susceptible to training. Older employees facing new job situations require specific training, as well as having need for development and growth opportunities.
6. Training needs require continuous monitoring.
7. The training officer of an agency is a professional with a responsibility to assist supervisors in solving training problems.

8. Many of the self-development steps important to the supervisor's own growth are equally important to the development of peers and subordinates. Knowledge of these is important when the supervisor consults with others on development and growth opportunities.

G. Health, Safety, and Accident Prevention

1. Management-minded supervisors take appropriate measures to assist employees in maintaining health and in assuring safe practices in the work environment.
2. Effective safety training and practices help to avoid injury and accidents.
3. Safety should be a management goal. All infractions of safety which are observed should be corrected without exception.
4. Employees' safety attitude, training and instruction, provision of safe tools and equipment, supervision, and leadership are considered highly important factors which contribute to safety and which can be influenced directly by supervisors.
5. When accidents do occur, they should be investigated promptly for very important reasons, including the fact that information which is gained can be used to prevent accidents in the future.

H. Equal Employment Opportunity

1. The supervisor should endeavor to treat all employees fairly, without regard to religion, race, sex, or national origin.
2. Groups tend to reflect the attitude of the leader. Prejudice can be detected even in very subtle form. Supervisors must strive to create a feeling of mutual respect and confidence in every employee.
3. Complete utilization of all human resources is a national goal. Equitable consideration should be accorded women in the work force, minority-group members, the physically and mentally handicapped, and the older employee. The important question is: "Who can do the job?"
4. Training opportunities, recognition for performance, overtime assignments, promotional opportunities, and all other personnel actions are to be handled on an equitable basis.

I. Improving Communications

1. Communications is achieving understanding between the sender and the receiver of a message. It also means sharing information—the creation of understanding.
2. Communication is basic to all human activity. Words are means of conveying meanings; however, real meanings are in people.
3. There are very practical differences in the effectiveness of one-way, impersonal, and two-way communications. Words spoken face-to-face are better understood. Telephone conversations are effective, but lack the rapport of person-to-person exchanges. The whole person communicates.
4. Cooperation and communication in an organization go hand in hand. When there is a mutual respect between people, spelling out rules and procedures for communicating is unnecessary.
5. There are several barriers to effective communications. These include failure to listen with respect and understanding, lack of skill in feedback, and misinterpreting the meanings of words used by the speaker. It is also common

practice to listen to what we want to hear, and tune out things we do not want to hear.

6. Communication is management's chief problem. The supervisor should accept the challenge to communicate more effectively and to improve interagency and intra-agency communications.
7. The supervisor may often plan for and conduct meetings. The planning phase is critical and may determine the success or the failure of a meeting.
8. Speaking before groups usually requires extra effort. Stage fright may never disappear completely, but it can be controlled.

J. Self-Development

1. Every employee is responsible for his own self-development.
2. Toastmaster and toastmistress clubs offer opportunities to improve skills in oral communications.
3. Planning for one's own self-development is of vital importance. Supervisors know their own strengths and limitations better than anyone else.
4. Many opportunities are open to aid the supervisor in his developmental efforts, including job assignments; training opportunities, both governmental and non-governmental—to include universities and professional conferences and seminars.
5. Programmed instruction offers a means of studying at one's own rate.
6. Where difficulties may arise from a supervisor's being away from his work for training, he may participate in televised home study or correspondence courses to meet his self-development needs.

K. Teaching and Training

1. The Teaching Process

Teaching is encouraging and guiding the learning activities of students toward established goals. In most cases this process consists of five steps: preparation, presentation, summarization, evaluation, and application.

a. Preparation

Preparation is two-fold in nature; that of the supervisor and the employee. Preparation by the supervisor is absolutely essential to success. He must know what, when, where, how, and whom he will teach. Some of the factors that should be considered are:

1) The objectives
2) The materials needed
3) The methods to be used
4) Employee participation
5) Employee interest
6) Training aids
7) Evaluation
8) Summarization

Employee preparation consists in preparing the employee to receive the material. Probably the most important single factor in the preparation of the employee is arousing and maintaining his interest. He must know the objectives of the training, why he is there, how the material can be used, and its importance to him.

b. Presentation
In presentation, have a carefully designed plan and follow it. The plan should be accurate and complete, yet flexible enough to meet situations as they arise. The method of presentation will be determined by the particular situation and objectives.

c. Summary
A summary should be made at the end of every training unit and program. In addition, there may be internal summaries depending on the nature of the material being taught. The important thing is that the trainee must always be able to understand how each part of the new material relates to the whole.

d. Application
The supervisor must arrange work so the employee will be given a chance to apply new knowledge or skills while the material is still clear in his mind and interest is high. The trainee does not really know whether he has learned the material until he has been given a chance to apply it. If the material is not applied, it loses most of its value.

e. Evaluation
The purpose of all training is to promote learning. To determine whether the training has been a success or failure, the supervisor must evaluate this learning.
In the broadest sense, evaluation includes all the devices, methods, skills, and techniques used by the supervisor to keep himself and the employees informed as to their progress toward the objectives they are pursuing. The extent to which the employee has mastered the knowledge, skills, and abilities, or changed his attitudes, as determined by the program objectives, is the extent to which instruction has succeeded or failed.
Evaluation should not be confined to the end of the lesson, day, or program but should be used continuously. We shall note later the way this relates to the rest of the teaching process.

2. Teaching Methods
A teaching method is a pattern of identifiable student and instructor activity used in presenting training material.
All supervisors are faced with the problem of deciding which method should be used at a given time.

a. Lecture
The lecture is direct oral presentation of material by the supervisor. The present trend is to place less emphasis on the trainer's activity and more on that of the trainee.

b. Discussion
Teaching by discussion or conference involves using questions and other techniques to arouse interest and focus attention upon certain areas, and by doing so creating a learning situation. This can be one of the most

valuable methods because it gives the employees an opportunity to express their ideas and pool their knowledge.

c. Demonstration
The demonstration is used to teach how something works or how to do something. It can be used to show a principle or what the results of a series of actions will be. A well-staged demonstration is particularly effective because it shows proper methods of performance in a realistic manner.

d. Performance
Performance is one of the most fundamental of all learning techniques or teaching methods. The trainee may be able to tell how a specific operation should be performed but he cannot be sure he knows how to perform the operation until he has done so.
As with all methods, there are certain advantages and disadvantages to each method.

e. Which Method to Use
Moreover, there are other methods and techniques of teaching. It is difficult to use any method without other methods entering into it. In any learning situation, a combination of methods is usually more effective than any one method alone.

Finally, evaluation must be integrated into the other aspects of the teaching-learning process.

It must be used in the motivation of the trainees; it must be used to assist in developing understanding during the training; and it must be related to employee application of the results of training.

This is distinctly the role of the supervisor.

www.ingramcontent.com/pod-product-compliance
Lightning Source LLC
Chambersburg PA
CBHW082043300426
44117CB00015B/2585